Images of Modern America

THE OHIO VALLEY JAZZ FESTIVAL

Front Cover: View of audience from stage of the festival in Riverfront Stadium, Cincinnati (SAA)

Upper Back Cover: Tour group in the stands of Riverfront Stadium (SAA)

Lower Back Cover (from left to right): Heritage Fair on Cincinnati's riverfront, 1988 (SAA), Luther Vandross performs at the Cincinnati festival (SAA), Front of house production at Riverfront Stadium, 1976 (SAA)

Images of Modern America

THE OHIO VALLEY JAZZ FESTIVAL

Scott M. Santangelo

ARCADIA PUBLISHING

ISBN 978-1-4671-2462-1

Published by Arcadia Publishing
Charleston, South Carolina

Printed in the United States of America

Library of Congress Control Number: 2016944693

For all general information, please contact Arcadia Publishing:
Telephone 843-853-2070
Fax 843-853-0044
E-mail sales@arcadiapublishing.com
For customer service and orders:
Toll-Free 1-888-313-2665

Visit us on the Internet at www.arcadiapublishing.com

In memory of Dino Santangelo's unique place in Cincinnati's entertainment industry and of his parents, Corradino and Jilda—an American success story.

Contents

ACKNOWLEDGMENTS

Thanks to the wonderful file keeping of the festival's Cincinnati office staff, a unique record of the history of the jazz festival has been preserved, from which much of the material presented in this book has been drawn. By arrangement with the Cincinnati Historical Library and Archives, the original files will be preserved as the Santangelo Agency Archive (SAA), enabling future research into this interesting and little-known chapter of the city's history. Unless otherwise attributed, all of the images within this publication were drawn from the agency's files.

Thanks are also due to those whose photographs so powerfully tell the festival story. A few special attributions are due, notably to Cincinnati photographers Mel Grier and Mike Mitchell, who had the foresight to capture many moments (big and small) that prove the maxim that "a picture is worth a thousand words." Good fortune and persistence led to the discovery of rare photographs from the French Lick and Carthage Fairground events, making it possible for these early concerts to be seen in context of the more advanced productions that would develop in later years.

An apology is in order to countless people who are not mentioned within this publication. Immediate family and many extended family members are given little recognition within these pages, and the list of others who should be mentioned could easily have filled another volume. Their contributions also deserve to be shared and appreciated. This apology must also extend to the necessarily incomplete (and occasionally erratic) timeline format, which imperfectly relates a complex history for which a caption format is simply inadequate.

The people of the Greater Cincinnati area also deserve recognition for their early enthusiasm and support for the jazz festival, which provided the spark that fueled its success. To those who live here, it will come as no surprise that the Midwest proved the most fertile ground for such a seed to take root. And finally, thanks to Dino Santangelo himself, whose irrepressible optimism, character, and talents were reflections of the best traits of the community he called home. Cincinnati is a better place for his contributions to it.

Introduction

To the delight of fans from across the country, the Ohio Valley Jazz Festival (OVJF) is a chapter of Cincinnati's entertainment history that is still celebrated every year. Known by many names over the decades, the festival is an annual fixture on the city's summer calendar, showcasing the nation's top R&B acts to diverse audiences. It is now held at the Paul Brown Stadium. Memories of the earliest concerts now belong to an older generation, themselves a reflection of a Cincinnati that has changed dramatically since the transformational 1960s, when black and white television and rotary phones were the norm, seat belts were optional, and many establishments were still segregated.

The first 25 years of the festival are the legacy of Cincinnati promoter Dino Santangelo (1933–1986), who brought the event to his hometown through the partnership he developed with Newport Jazz Festival founder George Wein. The two had a lot in common (both had been high school band leaders, composers, and musicians), and Wein's festival concept would find international acceptance through Santangelo's organizational genius. The event in Cincinnati quickly grew roots of its own, though at the beginning the concept of a jazz festival was a bit unsettling to the "squares" in the city's administration, who expressed their concerns for public safety.

On the whole, Cincinnati seemed an unlikely choice to host such an event in the early 1960s, but jazz music was wildly popular in the Midwest, and the Queen City was no exception. Many small but dedicated radio stations supported the format, and Cincinnati's WNOP, broadcasting from its floating "jazz ark" studio, was a beacon of nonconformity in an otherwise conservative media scene (Santangelo was a big fan of WNOP DJ Leo Underhill). The timing was perfect for an event that would reflect the shifting cultural landscape, and the jazz festival in 1962 was clearly that event. As the talent lineups evolved over the years toward mainstream R&B, the festivals bridged cultural divides and eased racial tensions through the common denominators of popular music and an undeniably positive economic impact.

Founded on such pillars, the jazz festivals quickly became a national (and international) success. At the time of his death in 1986, Santangelo was among the nation's leading specialists in the presentation of music festivals, pioneering techniques of multi-act stadium and coliseum production that became industry standards. While Santangelo's contributions to the Cincinnati entertainment scene are not confined to the festival, it is undoubtedly the event for which he will be best remembered.

One

1950–1960

The Early Years

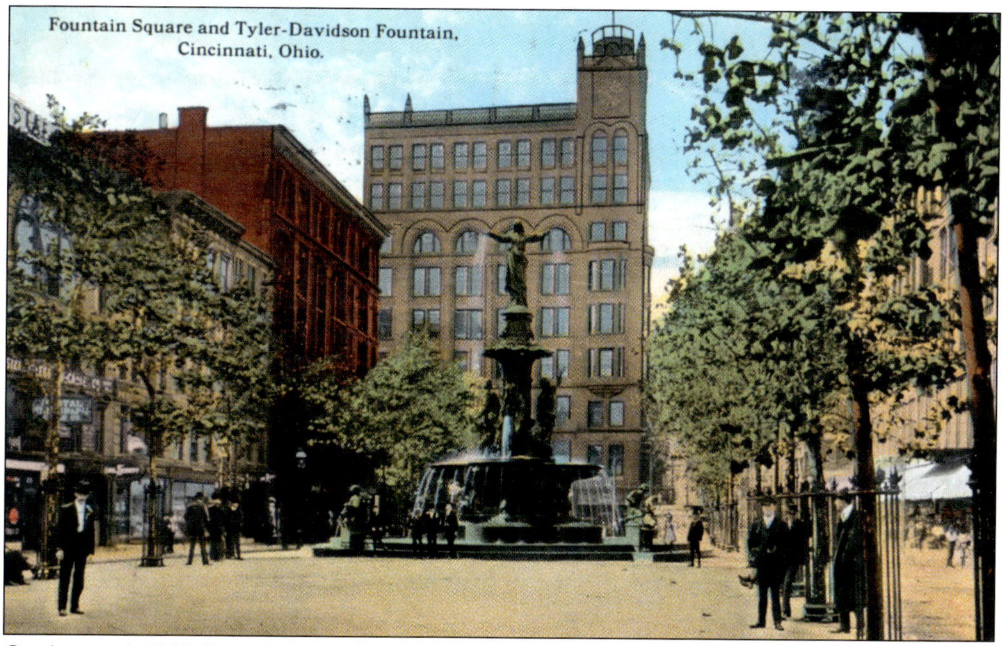

On August 4, 1913, Dino Santangelo's father, Corradino, at age 16, boarded the freighter *Hamburg*, bound from Naples, Italy, to New York City in the United States of America. Like thousands of other immigrants, he passed through Ellis Island on his way to stay with relatives in Cincinnati, Ohio. He became a skilled tailor, married Jilda Santoro, and raised a family of four in the blue-collar neighborhood of Hyde Park. Dino was the oldest, born on December 9, 1933.

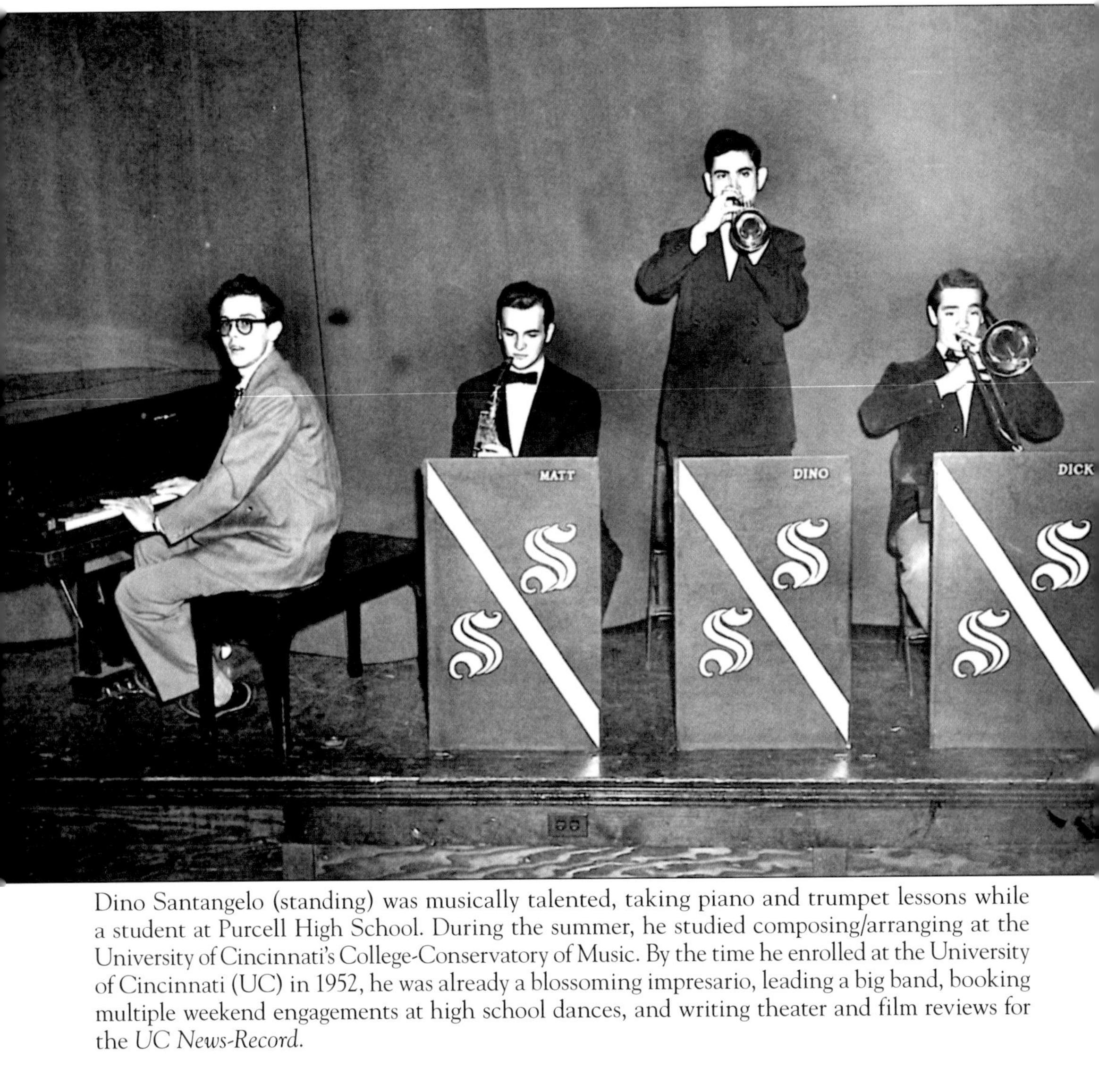

Dino Santangelo (standing) was musically talented, taking piano and trumpet lessons while a student at Purcell High School. During the summer, he studied composing/arranging at the University of Cincinnati's College-Conservatory of Music. By the time he enrolled at the University of Cincinnati (UC) in 1952, he was already a blossoming impresario, leading a big band, booking multiple weekend engagements at high school dances, and writing theater and film reviews for the *UC News-Record*.

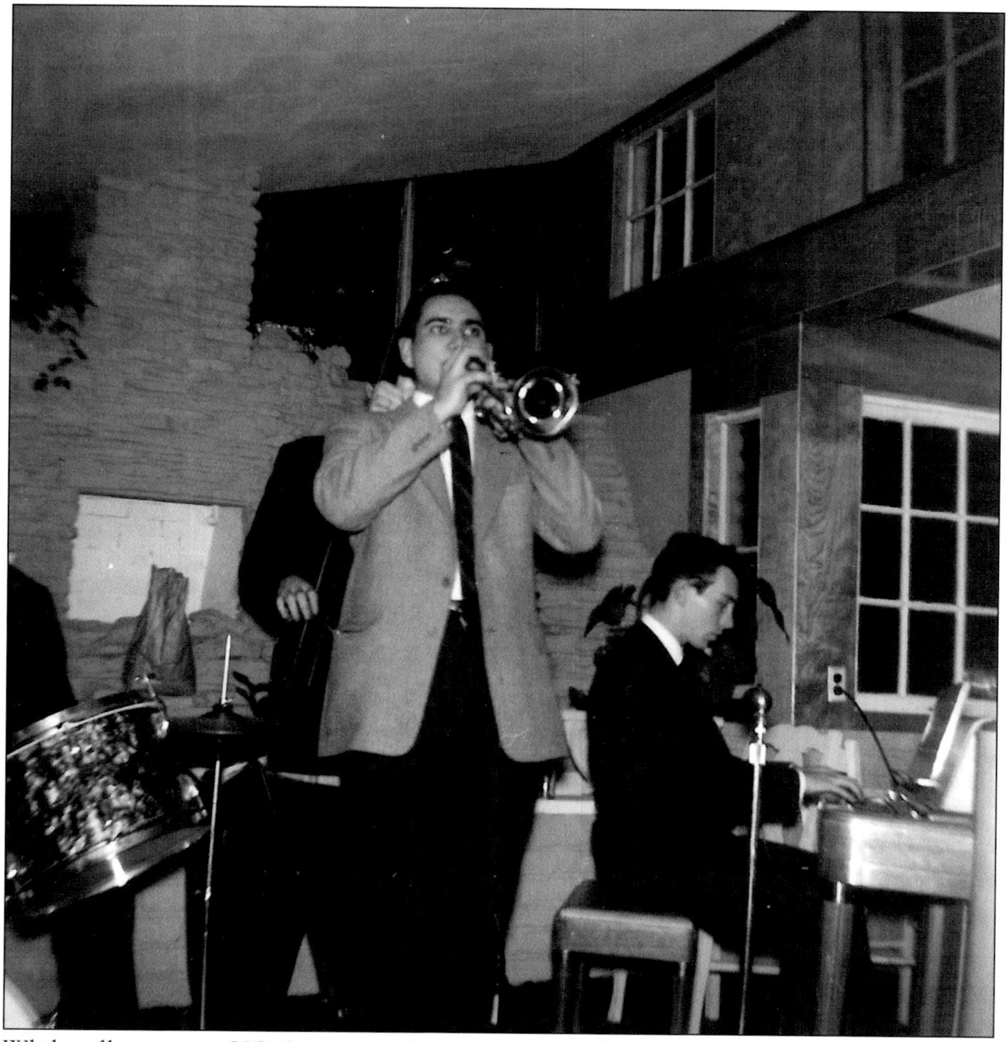

While still a junior at UC, Santangelo (playing trumpet above) answered an advertisement for a part-time press agent at the Sheraton-Gibson Hotel. The position was so new that no office space was available, requiring an expansive broom closet be converted into Santangelo's new office. "Room 125" gave him a prestigious downtown address. He quickly became the Sheraton's Midwestern public relations specialist, handling openings of new hotels, restaurants, and entertainment facilities like the Beverly Hills Supper Club. Santangelo described himself at the time as a "self-employed public relations counselor."

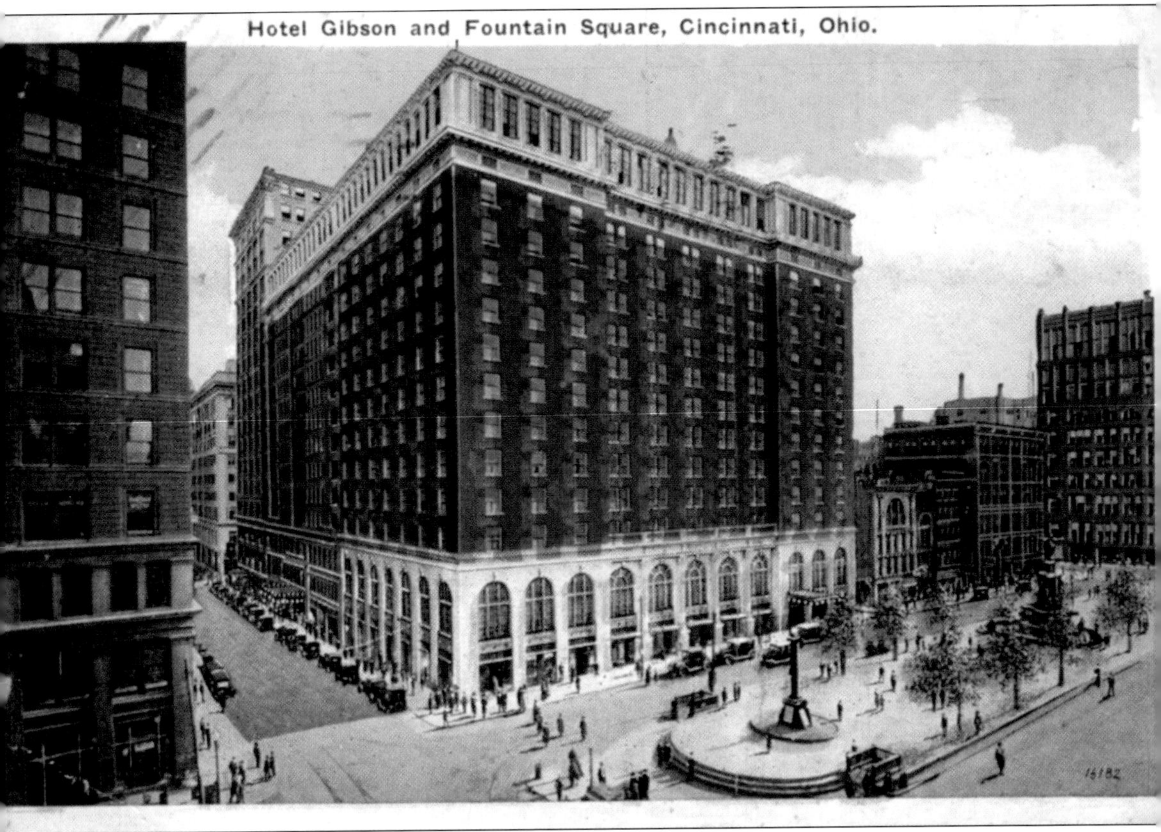

The Hotel Gibson was renowned as a Cincinnati institution, founded in 1849 at the corner of Fifth and Walnut Streets. Expanded in 1914 and again in 1922, the hotel was famous for its Louis XVI ballroom, grand stairway, and Fountain and Florentine rooms. The Florentine was known as "America's most beautiful dining room." The Sheraton Corporation acquired the property in 1950, and it was thereafter known as the Sheraton-Gibson. Celebrities frequented the hotel, and Santangelo recalled meeting Sammy Davis Jr. when he stayed at the hotel during his engagement at the Beverly Hills Supper Club. After a long day of interviews, Davis surprised him by saying, "Come on, Dino, let's go shopping!" Visiting several stores in downtown Cincinnati, Davis would go to the counters and shake hands, "shopping" all afternoon and signing hundreds of autographs in three hours. It was an early lesson in how to promote personal appearances. The 1970s saw the demolition of the Gibson, along with the Albee Theater and the Fountain esplanade, which had previously defined the heart and center of Cincinnati's downtown.

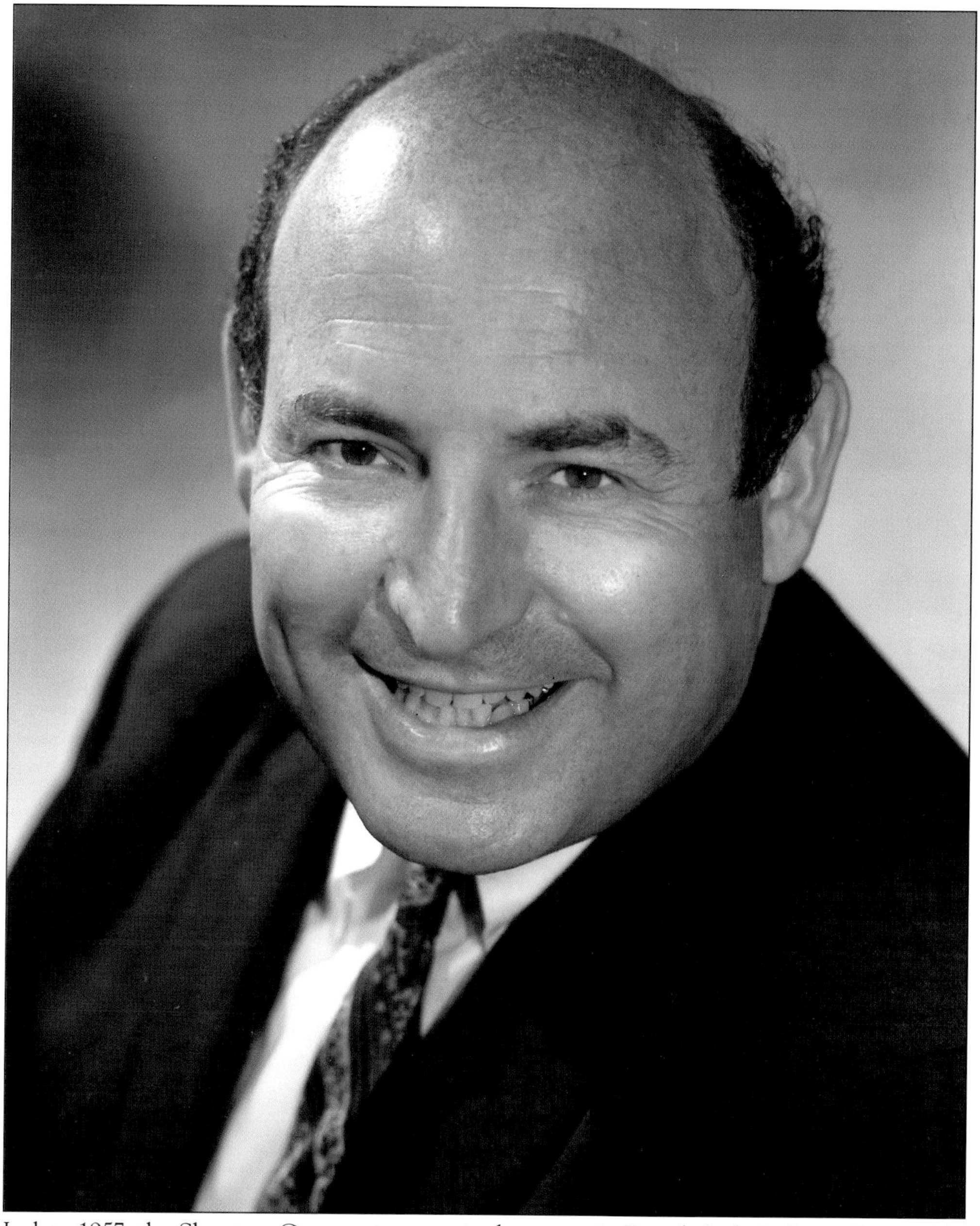

In late 1957, the Sheraton Corporation acquired a resort in French Lick, Indiana. Santangelo devised a series of outdoor concerts to attract visitors from nearby metropolitan areas, and initial projects for the new hotel promotion included a presentation of Arthur Fiedler and the Boston Pops Orchestra and a weekend Country Music Festival. Encouraged by the success of these shows, Santangelo pursued the concept of bringing an annual event to the Sheraton: "I went [to the French Lick Sheraton] with Al Banks, who was director of entertainment for Sheraton. We hit upon the idea of a jazz festival and, of course, at that time there was only one Jazz Festival in existence and that was at Newport. We had both heard of George Wein, and Al Banks had met him. So we contacted George and put on the Festival." The timing could not have been better for Wein (pictured above), and the Newport spark would catch fire in the Midwest.

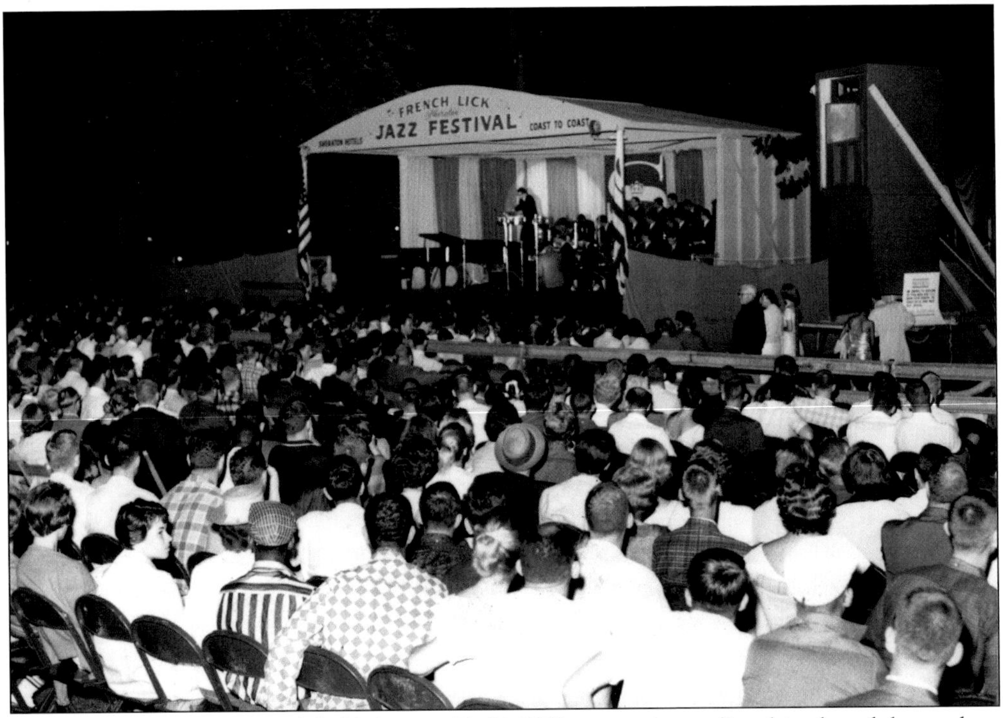

The French Lick Jazz Festival, held August 15–17, 1958, was an immediate hit, though by modern standards the production levels were rather spartan. Using a corner of the resort's golf course, the three-day program presented a constellation of stars, including David Baker (pictured below), Edward "Duke" Ellington, Louis Armstrong, Gene Kruppa, Gerry Mulligan, Dizzy Gillespie, Roy Eldridge, Miles Davis, the Four Freshman, Erroll Garner, Eddie Condon, Stan Kenton, and Anita O'Day. The fledgling festival unfortunately became the victim of its own success, as the hotel and the area surrounding it were unable to meet the demand for rooms and other services required by such a major outdoor event. The French Lick Jazz Festival was cancelled in 1959, and a concert in Evansville, Indiana, was hurriedly substituted for the talent already purchased. (Both, courtesy of the French Lick Sheraton.)

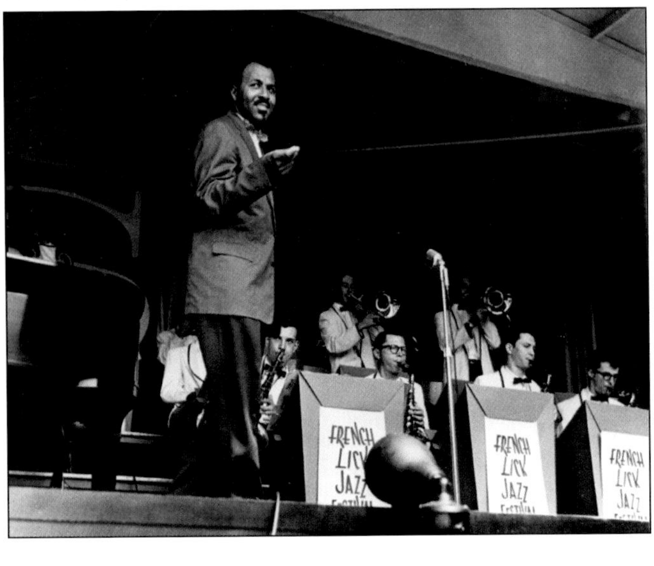

Two

1961–1965

The First Cincinnati Festivals

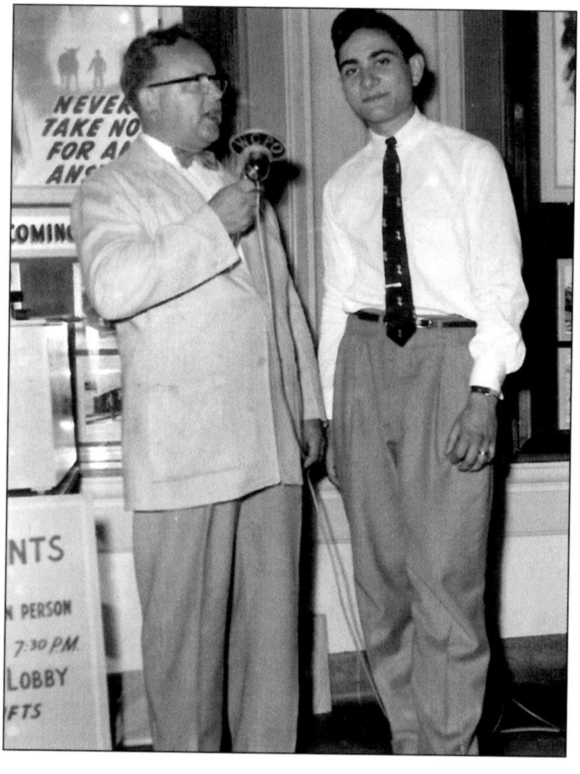

Cincinnati has traditionally been supportive of all things musical, and jazz was no exception when it hit the airwaves and the club scene in the late 1950s. WNOP-AM led the local radio charge with colorful programming from the station's signature floating studio, the "jazz ark." Leo Underhill (left) was one of the station's most colorful announcers, known for substituting bar closings for school closings during inclement weather, and his on-air irreverence was the stuff of legend. WNOP's quirky appeal was irresistible and contributed to the early foothold the jazz festival gained in Cincinnati. Santangelo's (at right in the photograph with an unidentified local announcer) regional advertising and promotional strategies capitalized on the phenomenon, working with stations in nearby markets to attract audiences from hundreds of miles away.

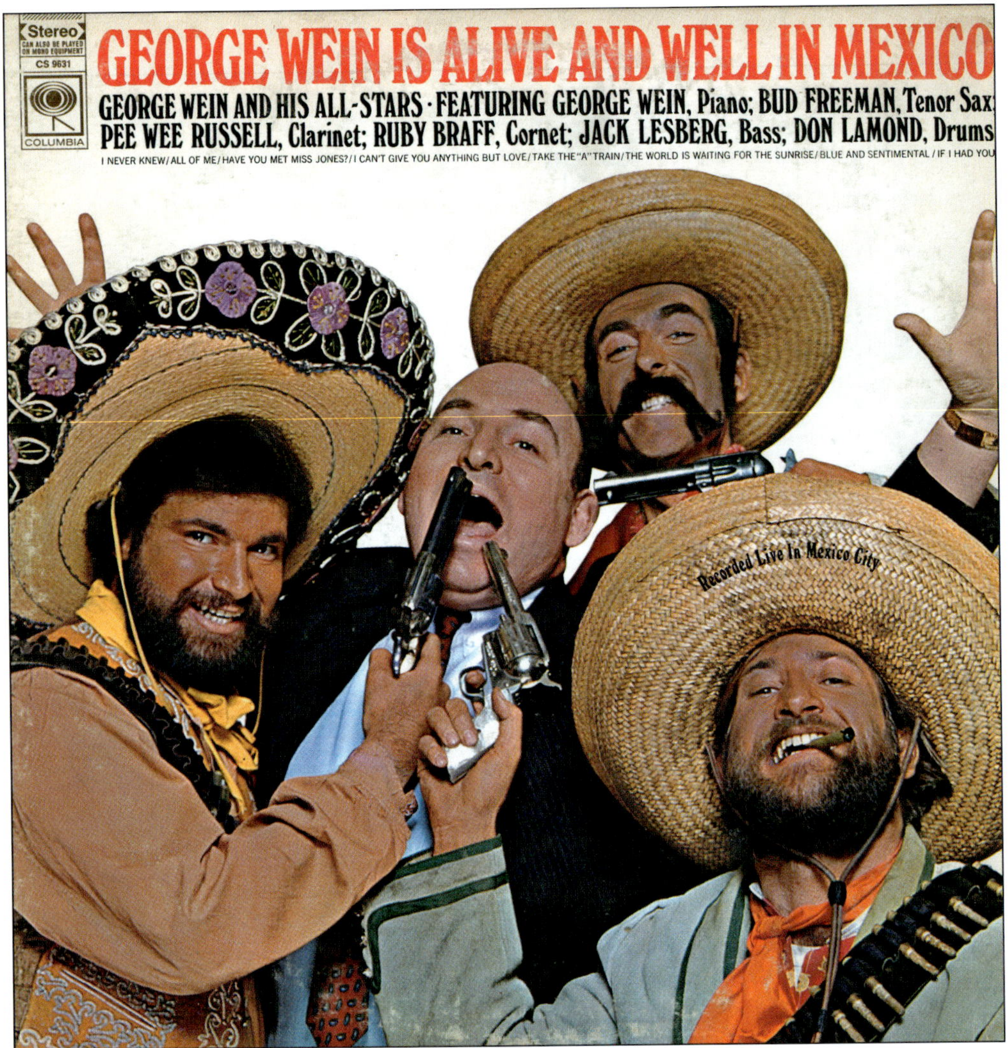

In addition to his talent as an impresario, George Wein is a fine jazz pianist. George Wein and his All Stars were a regular feature in festival lineups, though the composition of the All Stars would change frequently. The album *George Wein Is Alive And Well In Mexico* is representative of the ensemble's key players, featuring Bud Freeman on tenor sax, Pee Wee Russell on clarinet, Ruby Braff on cornet, Jack Lesberg on bass, and Don Lamond on drums. Wein's personal relationships with virtually all of the leading jazz players of the day made the incredible lineup of festival performers possible.

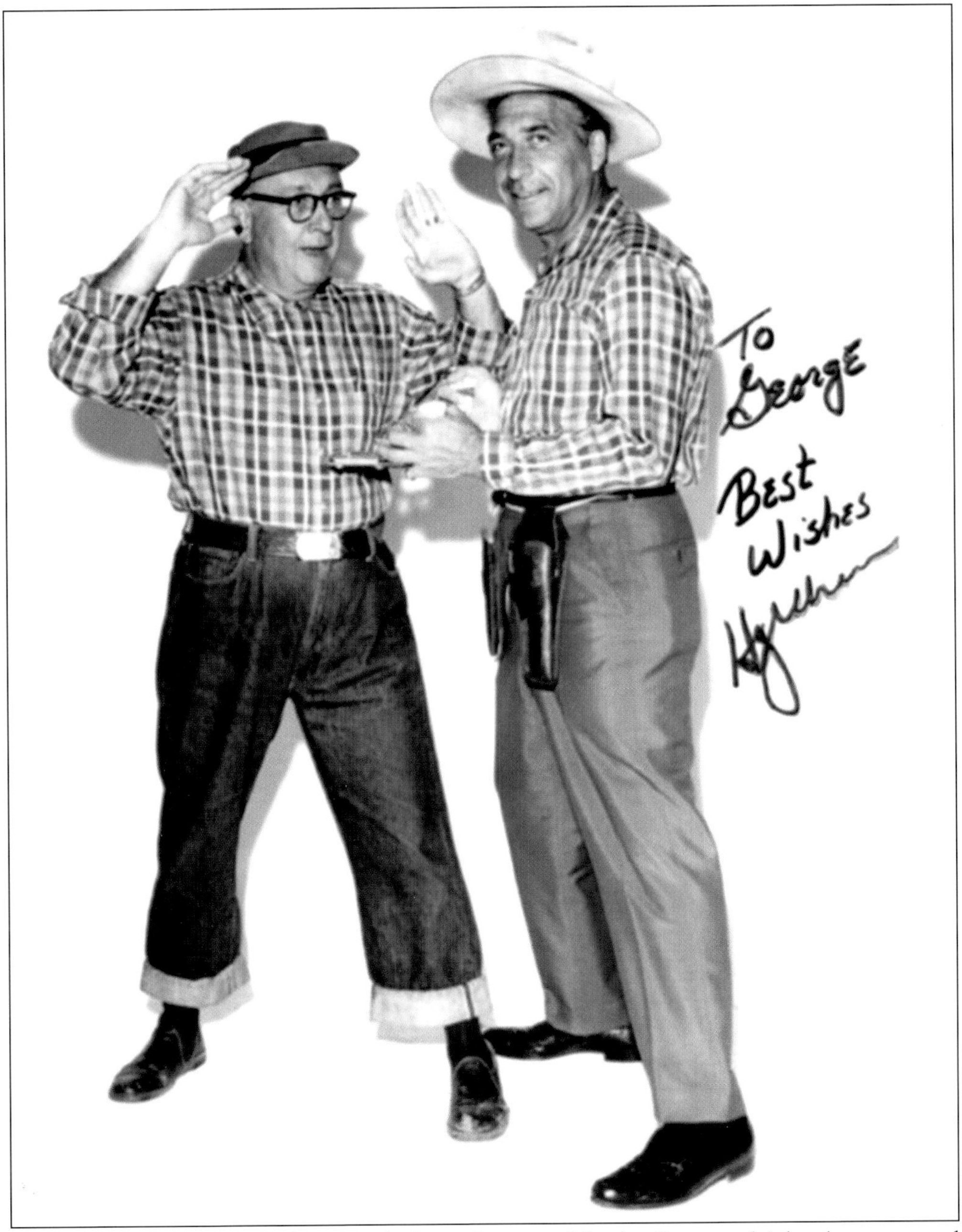

Complementing Wein's familiarity with the performers of the day, Santangelo's local contacts and clients provided the financial backing necessary to produce the festival in Cincinnati. Within the city's creative business community, Santangelo found early believers in the event. One investor, Hyman "Hy" Ullner (right), was the founder of local department store Rinks and better known as its television spokesman under the guise of "the Bargain City Kid." He also hosted WCPO-TV's popular *Shock Theater* movie program in Cincinnati, along with sidekick Willie Thrall (left).

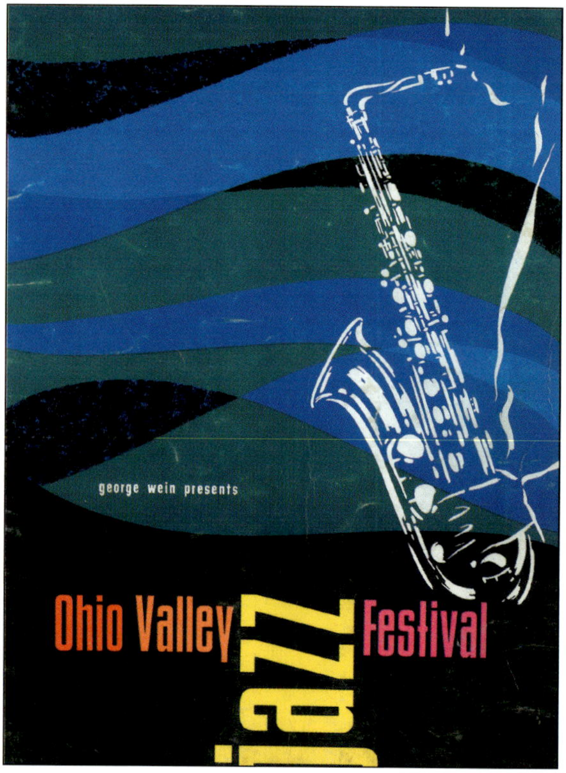

In contrast to the attitude of the police chief and the city manager, local media and celebrities from across the region enthusiastically supported the festival. Television pioneer Ruth Lyons featured Duke Ellington on her popular *50/50 Club* that year. A young boxer named Cassius Clay attended the festival and persuaded George Wein to let him to read his poem ("out in four!") to promote his upcoming fight with Archie Moore. Local theater critic E.B. Radcliffe saluted Santangelo's persistence in bringing the Newport Jazz Festival to Cincinnati, even though it might not have appealed to his personal aesthetic. His review "Dino's Cadenzas Count" (*Cincinnati Enquirer*, August 15, 1962) summed up the genuine support of the local gentry: "So here's a toast in vino, for good old Dino. He's got Cincinnati with it again. That's the way they put it in the bombazine-clad squared circles in which I waltz clog." (Courtesy of William Hammond.)

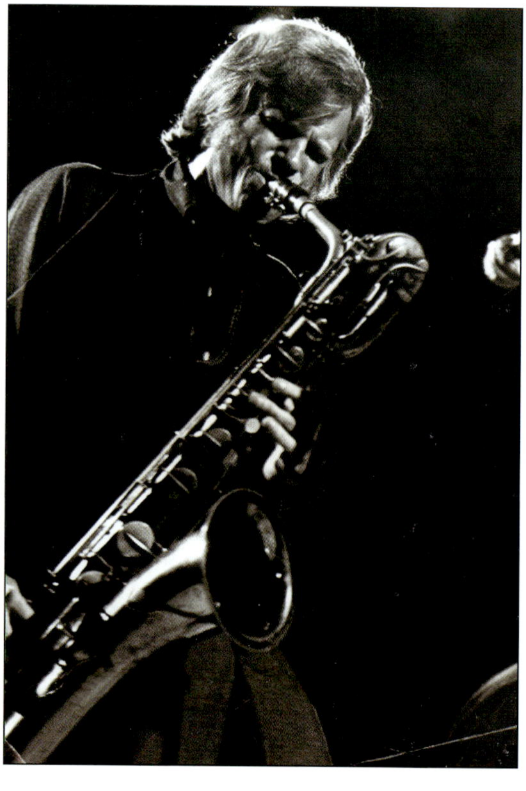

The event at the Carthage Fairgrounds in 1962, the first jazz festival in Cincinnati, was officially titled the Ohio Valley Jazz Festival. Held on the weekend of August 24–26, the lineup included jazz greats Louis Armstrong, Dave Brubeck, Edward "Duke" Ellington, Joe Williams, Horace Silver, Marshall Brown, Ruby Braff, Pee Wee Russell, Coleman Hawkins, Roy Eldridge, Jimmy Smith, Gerry Mulligan (right), Sonny Rollins, Jack Teagarden, Ahmad Jamal, and Carmen McRae. Tickets were a modest $5, $4.25, and $3.50, and as they had at French Lick, people came from miles around to see the shows. The fair board was vindicated by the outcome, and a letter to the Board of County Commissioners boasted that "this affair was a huge success . . . well attended and conducted without any trouble."

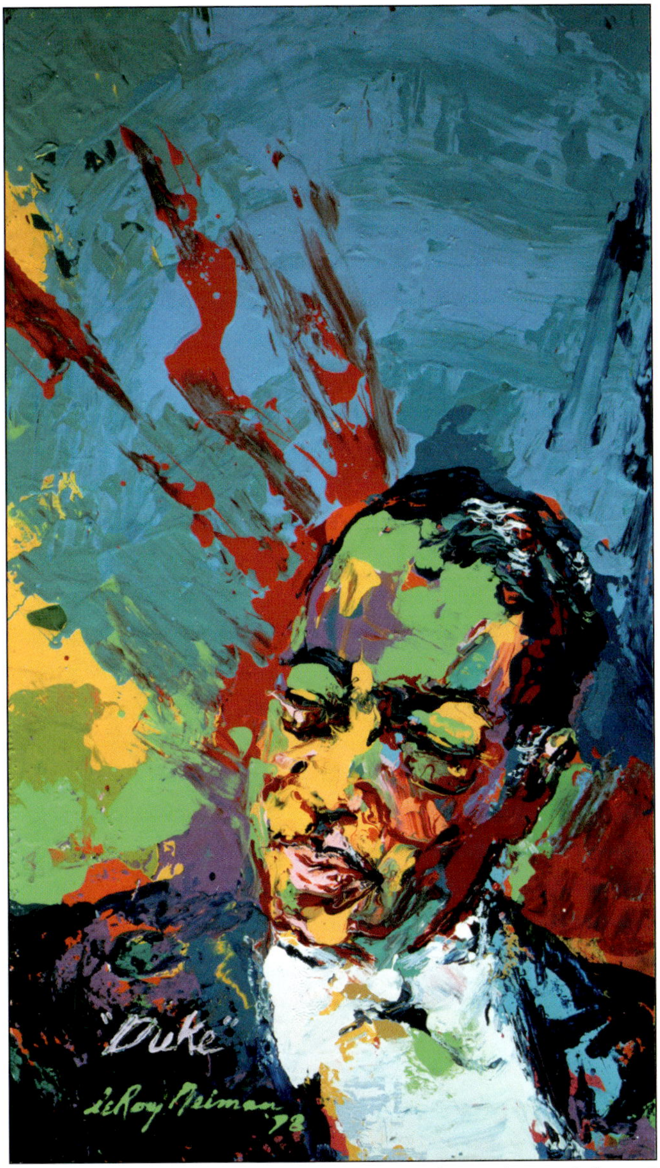

The limitations of Carthage Fairgrounds were apparent and went beyond the rickety grandstands. It was again time to move the event, but this time to a larger, more capable, and centrally located venue. Crosley Field was the home of the Cincinnati Reds in downtown Cincinnati and well equipped to handle large crowds. Facilities management was eager to host the popular event, and the 3rd Annual Ohio Valley Jazz Festival was held there in 1964. On Friday, August 14, audiences saw the Dee Felice Trio, Lou Rawls, Count Basie, Chet Baker, Aretha Franklin, and Louis Armstrong. Saturday's show featured Dizzy Gillespie, Gloria Lynne, Edward "Duke" Ellington, Bunny Briggs, the Dave Brubeck Quartet with Paul Desmond, and John Coltrane. Sunday's show closed out the weekend with the Abersold-Hoffman Septet, Thelonious Monk, Jimmy Smith, Stan Getz and Astrud Gilberto, Woody Herman, and the Newport Jazz Festival All Stars (Ruby Braff, Bud Freeman, George Wein, Alex Cirin, and Phil Paul). Lynne and Coltrane were no-shows; it was a valuable lesson the festival promoters took to heart, and future bookings required detailed itineraries.

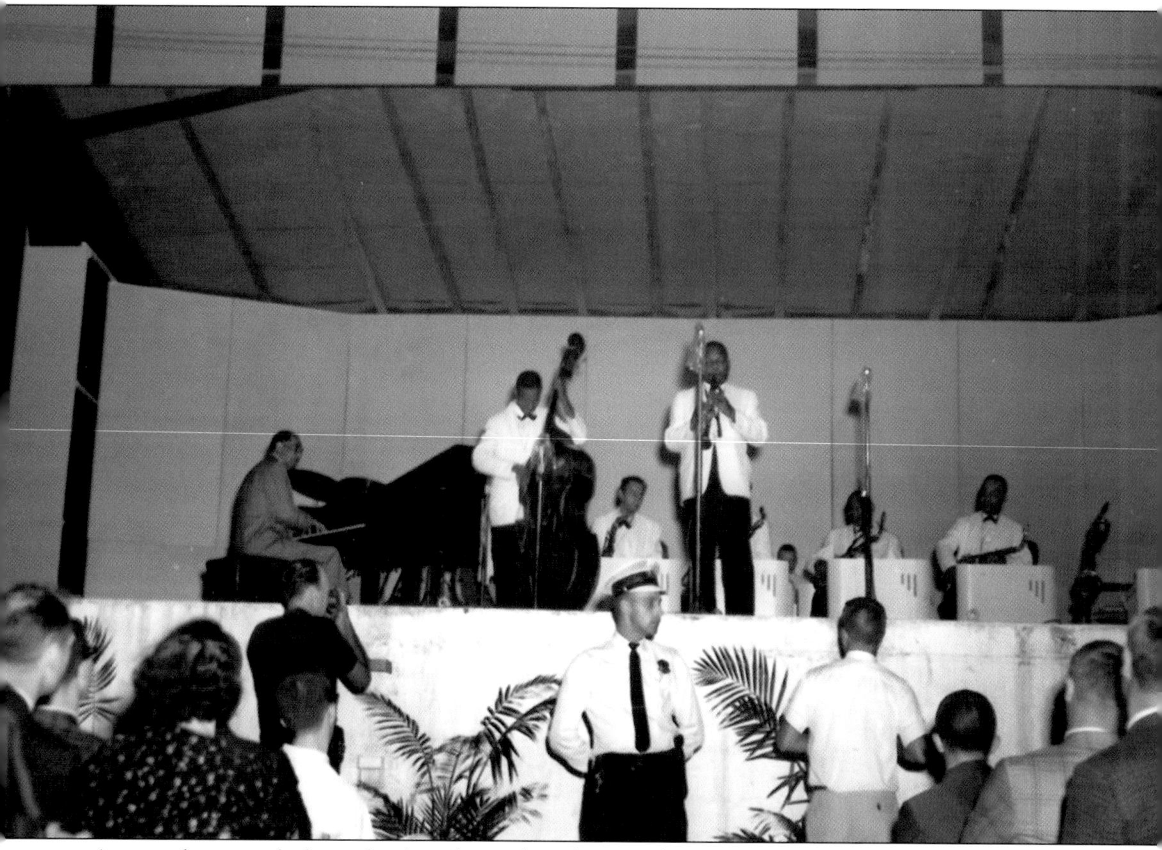

A rare photograph from the first festival at the Carthage Fairground is shown above. Duke Ellington is seen at the piano, leading his orchestra for early festival fans. The festival offered a unique platform for performers that might have otherwise struggled for an opportunity to be heard. Duke Ellington's festival contract in 1964 came with a clear caveat—"It is mutually agreed and understood between all parties concerned that the artist or artists have prerogative of cancelling this contract if in any instance an audience is segregated because of race or color." (Courtesy of William Hammond.)

Three

1966–1969

National Tours

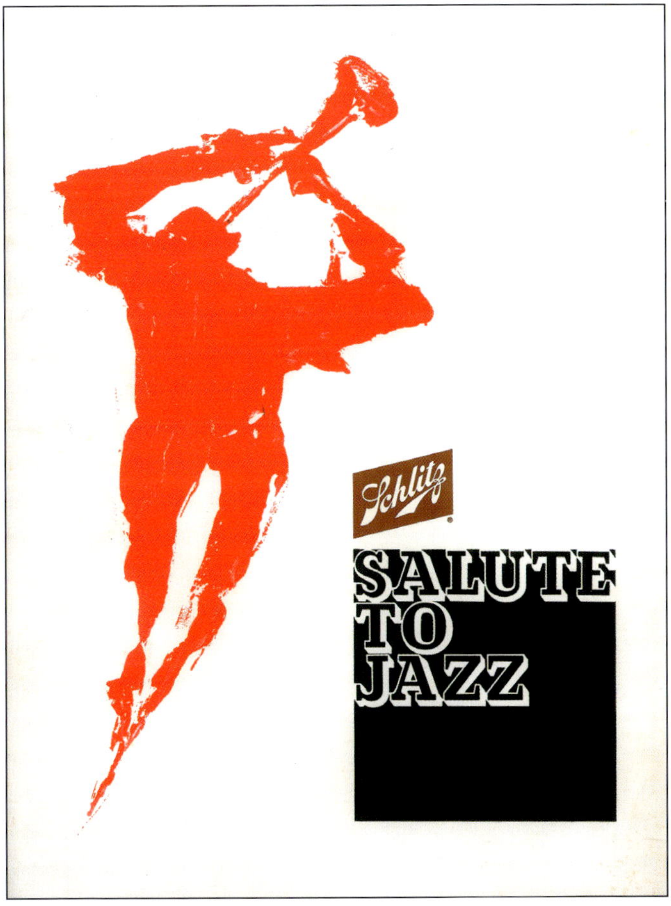

The 6th Annual Ohio Valley Jazz Festival was held on August 5, 1967, at Crosley Field and featured Jimmy Smith, Cannonball Adderley, Nina Simone, Herbie Mann, Ramsey Lewis, and Dizzy Gillespie. Tickets cost $5, $4, $3.25, and $2.50. In an article in the *Troy Daily News*, Bruce George noted that "this year is unusual because the artists are not only giants in jazz, but are commercially popular. This means that even those who do not 'dig' far out sounds, as well as the 'in' people will find themselves together in full pleasure this year."

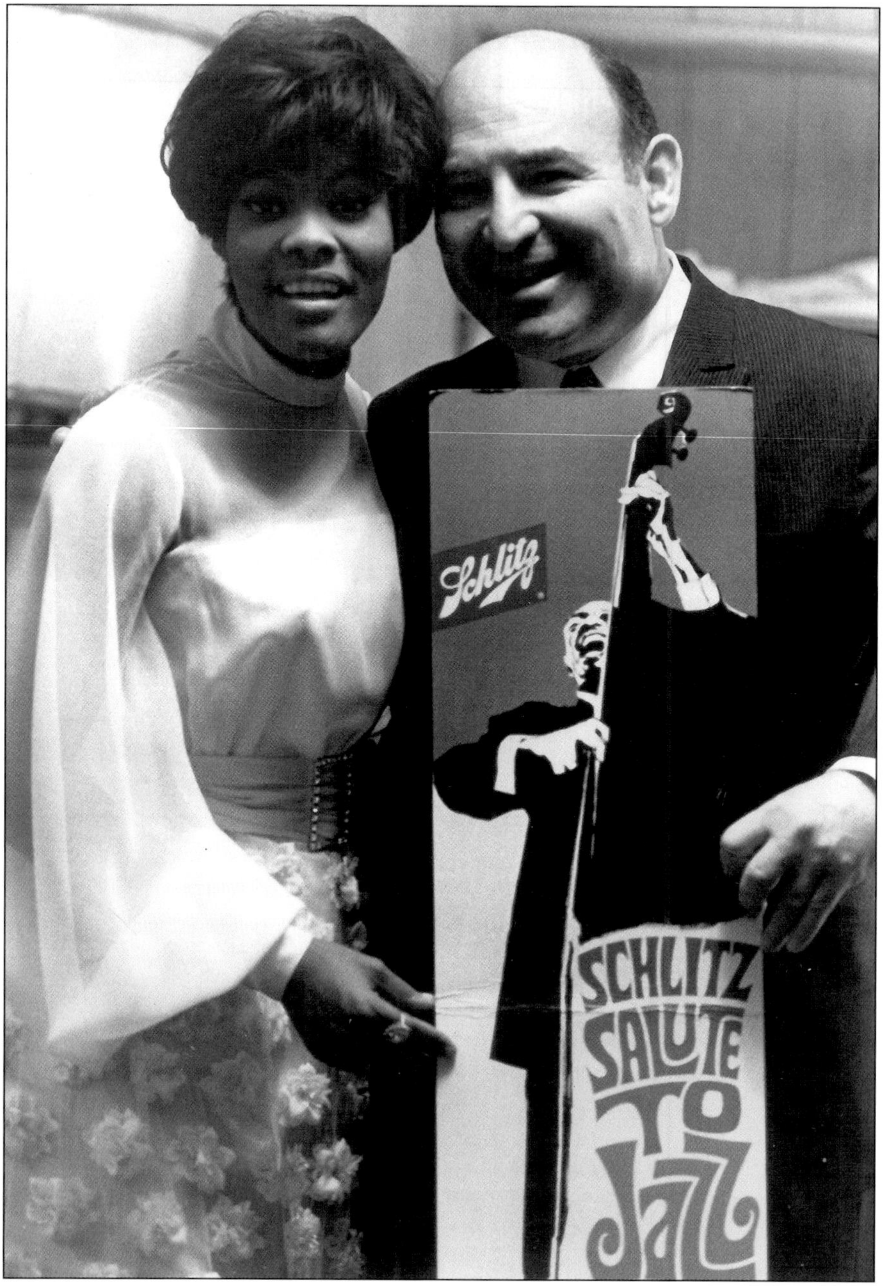

The 7th Annual Ohio Valley Jazz Festival in 1968 at Crosley Field showcased Dionne Warwick (seen above with George Wein), Hugh Masekela, the Ramsey Lewis Trio, the Thelonious Monk Quartet, the Herbie Mann Quintet, and the Gary Burton Quartet. Under the "Schlitz Salute To Jazz" banner, festival events were produced in Winston-Salem, Nashville, Pittsburgh, Hampton, Atlanta, Newport, Dallas, Austin, Houston, Omaha, Denver, Oklahoma City, Phoenix, Oakland, San Diego, Rochester, Madison Detroit, Kansas City, St. Louis, Cleveland, Chicago, and Memphis. The Cincinnati festival closed a national tour that had begun almost a month earlier. Santangelo's Cincinnati offices would relocate to a modern business suite at 2260 Park Avenue, which served as the Festival National Press Headquarters.

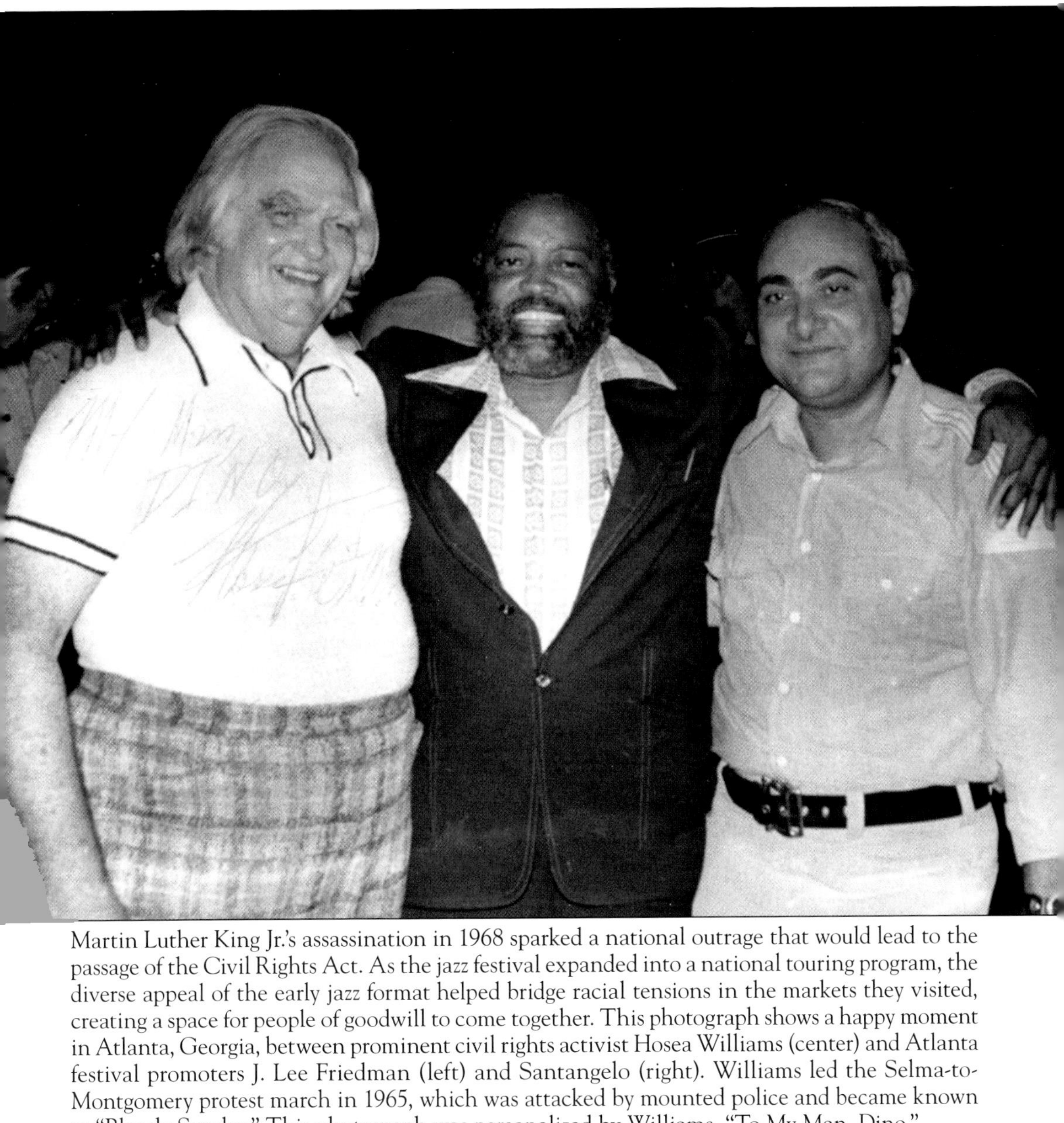

Martin Luther King Jr.'s assassination in 1968 sparked a national outrage that would lead to the passage of the Civil Rights Act. As the jazz festival expanded into a national touring program, the diverse appeal of the early jazz format helped bridge racial tensions in the markets they visited, creating a space for people of goodwill to come together. This photograph shows a happy moment in Atlanta, Georgia, between prominent civil rights activist Hosea Williams (center) and Atlanta festival promoters J. Lee Friedman (left) and Santangelo (right). Williams led the Selma-to-Montgomery protest march in 1965, which was attacked by mounted police and became known as "Bloody Sunday." This photograph was personalized by Williams, "To My Man, Dino."

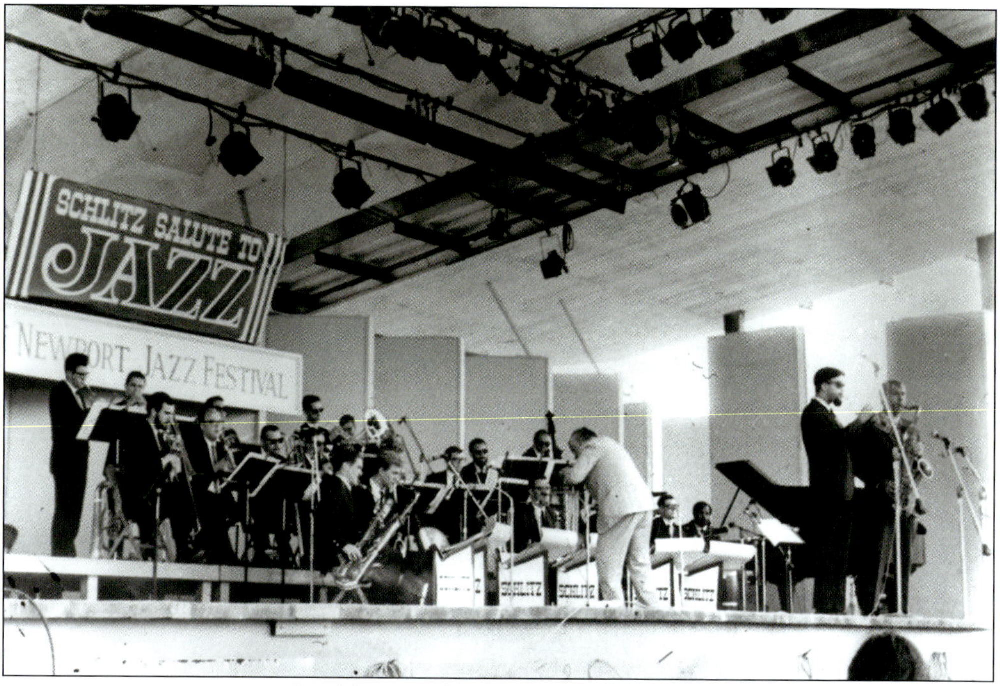

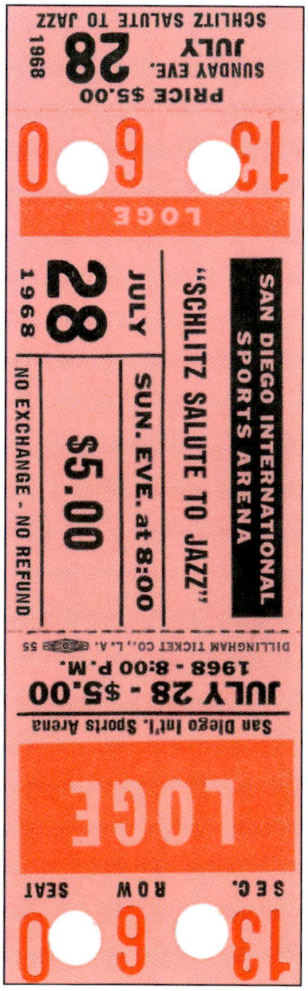

In addition to his other projects, Dino assisted in marketing Wein's Newport Jazz Festival. He outlined a national advertising campaign to enhance the event's identity and, citing the Cincinnati festival as a model, further detailed a promotional strategy to leverage the goodwill and participation of regional media. Attracted to this sort of exposure, major corporations began expressing interest in the proposals being circulated by Santangelo's office. The Newport brand was adapted to suit the needs of sponsors and reflected in everything from print and radio advertisements to event tickets (seen at left).

Four

1970–1975

Production Catches Up

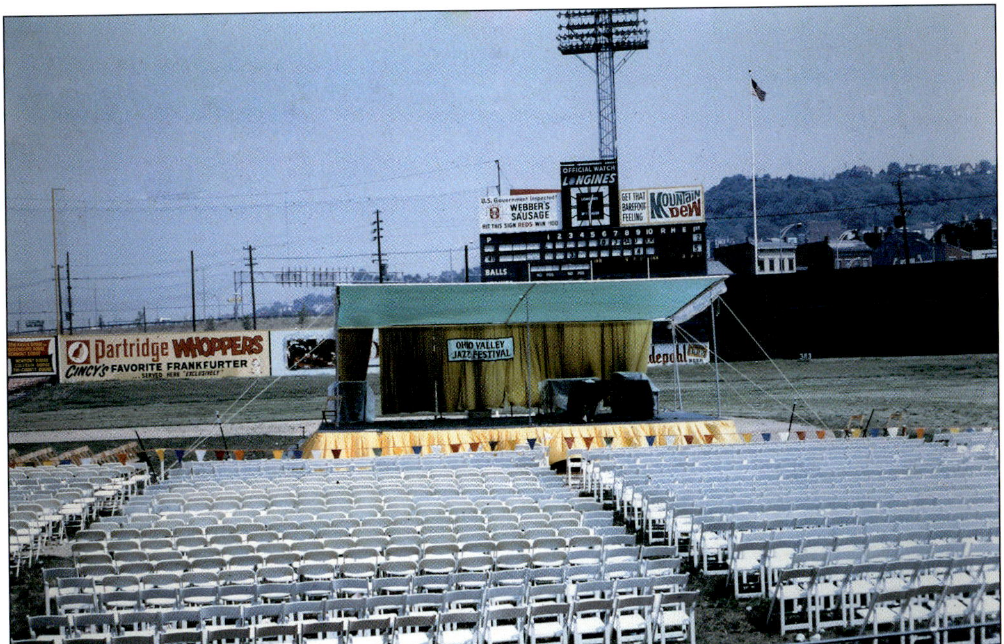

The 9th Annual Ohio Valley Jazz Festival took place in 1970. It marked the last time the festival was held at Crosley Field. The lineup was stellar on Saturday, August 15, with the Kenny Burrell Quartet, Gene Ammons & Sonny Stitt, Roberta Flack, the Eddie Harris Quartet, the Cannonball Adderley Quintet, the Les McCann Quartet, and the Herbie Mann Quintet. Sunday's show featured the Jimmy Smith Trio, Bobby "Blue" Bland, Tony Williams Lifeline, the Buddy Rich Orchestra, Mongo Santamaria & Band, and El Chicano. Attracting 26,500 people over two days, the Saturday night concert was sold out.

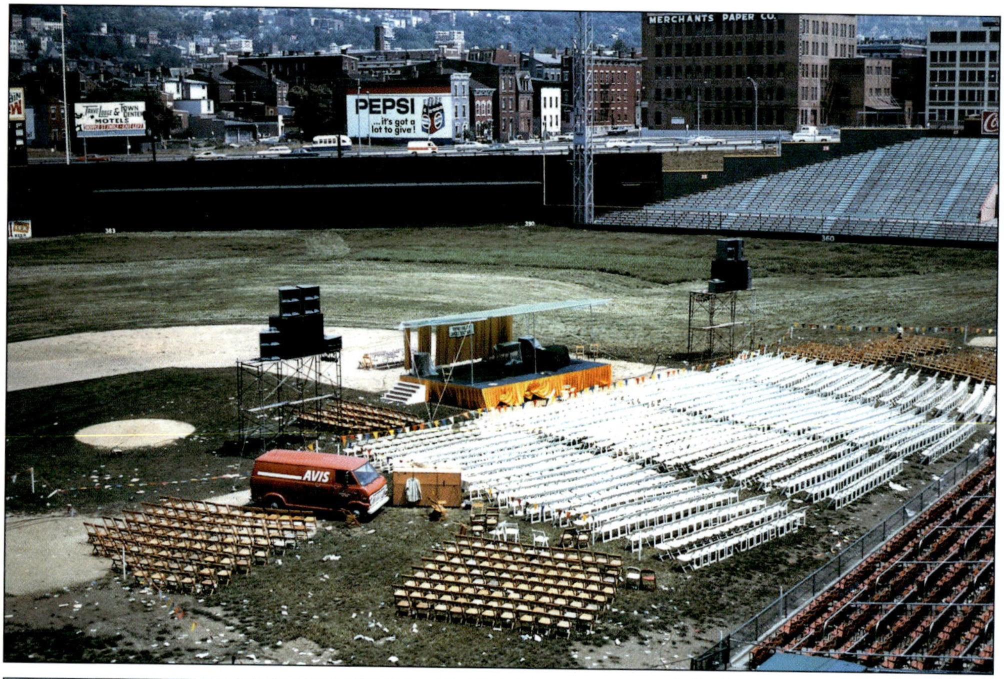

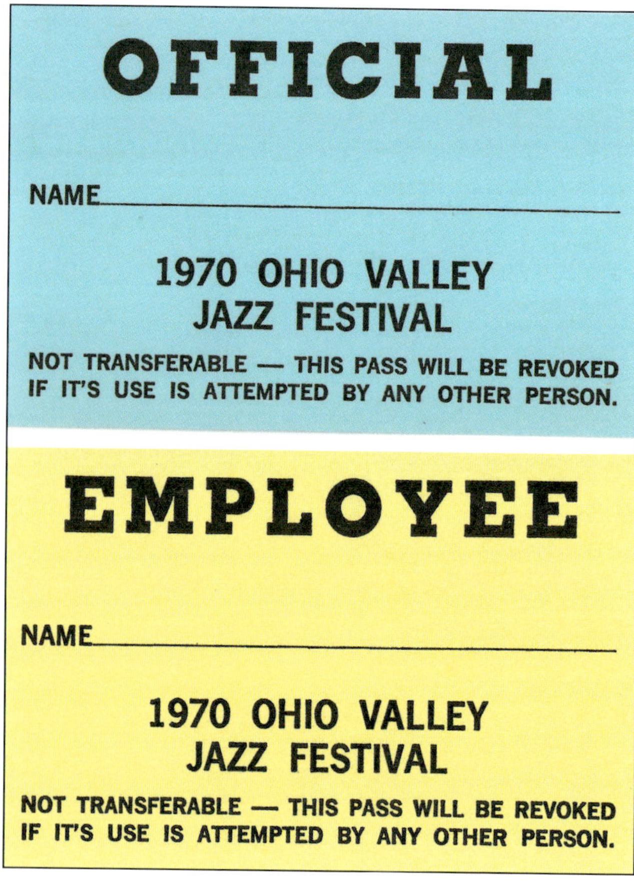

OFFICIAL

NAME______________________________

1970 OHIO VALLEY JAZZ FESTIVAL

NOT TRANSFERABLE — THIS PASS WILL BE REVOKED IF IT'S USE IS ATTEMPTED BY ANY OTHER PERSON.

EMPLOYEE

NAME______________________________

1970 OHIO VALLEY JAZZ FESTIVAL

NOT TRANSFERABLE — THIS PASS WILL BE REVOKED IF IT'S USE IS ATTEMPTED BY ANY OTHER PERSON.

Bob Bennett captured beautiful images of the festival's last year at Crosley Field (including the image shown above). He and Bill Hanley provided sound systems to the early festivals. Hanley is considered the "father of festival sound" and is best known for providing the sound system for the famous concert at Woodstock. Bennett had stayed to adjust the sound system the day before the show in Cincinnati, but as the sun set, the sound of insects in the tall, uncut grass grew louder and louder. Bennett called Santangelo and informed him of the problem—which he could hear over the phone. The next day, the grass was cut, and the field was sprayed to eliminate the noisy insects. Like the sound systems, backstage passes would also be developed to meet the needs of the event. Two examples from the 1970 festival in Cincinnati are shown at left.

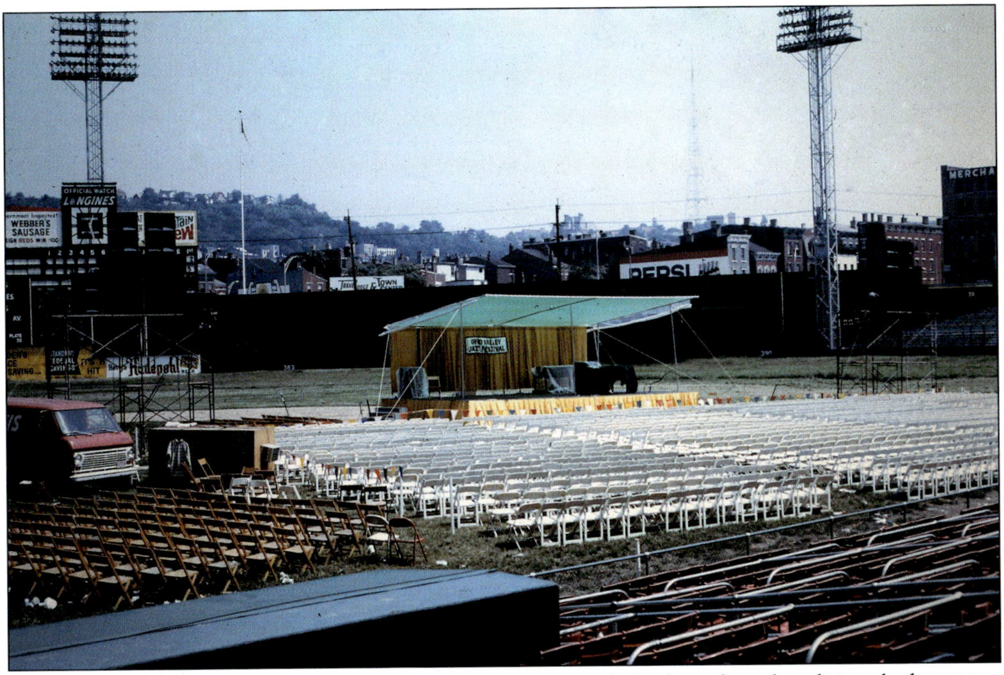

From the earliest days of the festival in Cincinnati, Santangelo had combined traditional advertising with clever marketing. An early strategy was to create a special press area and provide free tickets and credentials to virtually any legitimate media outlet that made a request to cover the event. The festival received several dozen such requests every year, from college radio DJs, regional newspapers, magazines, talk shows, and many other media outlets. This goodwill campaign translated into significant additional promotional exposure before and after the event. Despite complaints by critics that the press section was right in front of the speakers, they consistently gave the event high marks. Bruce George, music critic for the *Troy Daily News*, attended the jazz festival in 1970 and noted how smoothly the event had run: "The only freaks were a few white youths . . . also there to hear and dig jazz. There were no arrests for drugs, disturbing the peace, assaulting police etc. The only problem was getting and holding onto your seat."

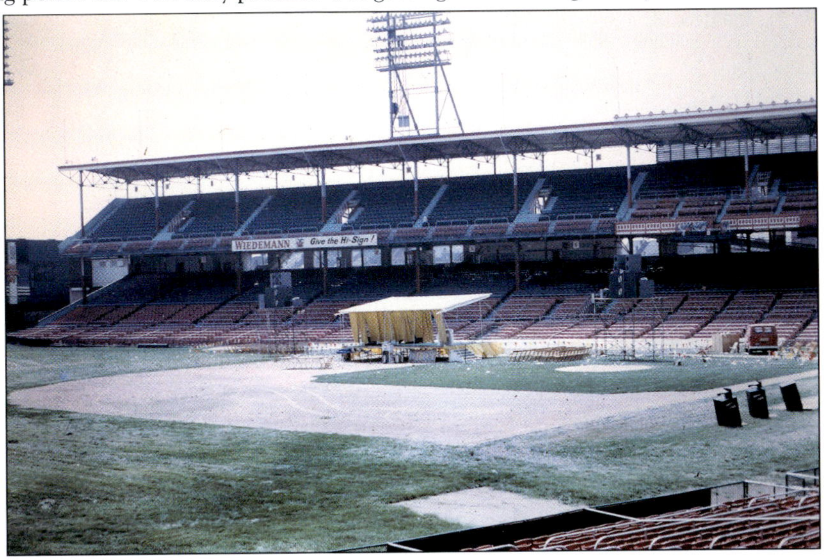

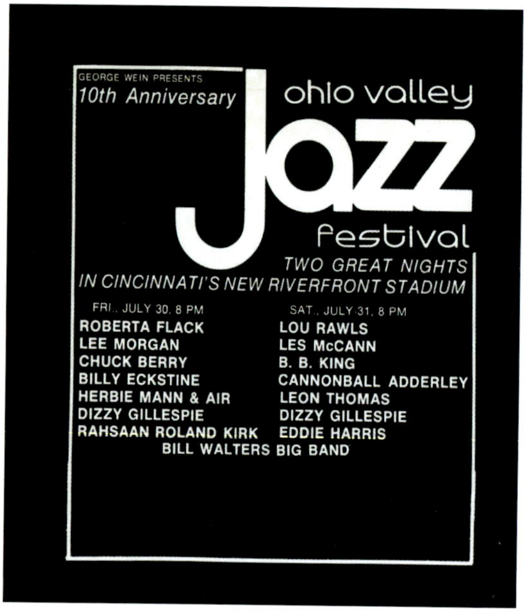

The 10th anniversary event was the first of many at the newly constructed Riverfront Stadium, and it featured a blend of old and new formats. On Friday, July 30, patrons saw Roberta Flack, the Lee Morgan Quintet, Chuck Berry, Billy Eckstein, the Herbie Mann Quintet, Dizzy Gillespie, and Rahsaan Roland Kirk & the Vibration Society. Saturday's lineup included Lou Rawls, the Les McCann Trio, B.B. King, Cannonball Adderley Quintet, and Leon Thomas & Band.

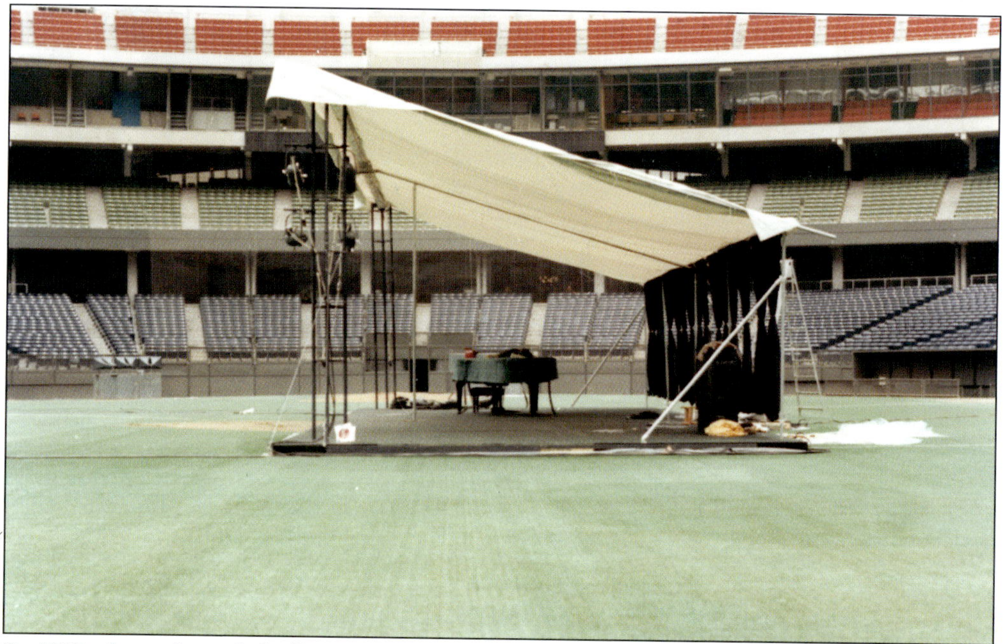

By 1971, the technical challenges associated with stadium settings required new production solutions. The venues were physically larger and required more careful treatment of the playing fields. Photographs from that year show staging reminiscent of the Crosley Field setup, which proved too small for Riverfront Stadium. Despite its size, the new venue created a dramatic backdrop for the festival, and the popular field seating maintained a surprising degree of intimacy. The festival built upon its experiences to customize its own touring package, complete with staging, sound, lights, and video. Field seating was essential to connecting the audience to the performers and required a variety of strategies to implement. Protecting the valuable turf was a priority for stadium management, who required various types of covers—typically plywood sheets covered with canvas.

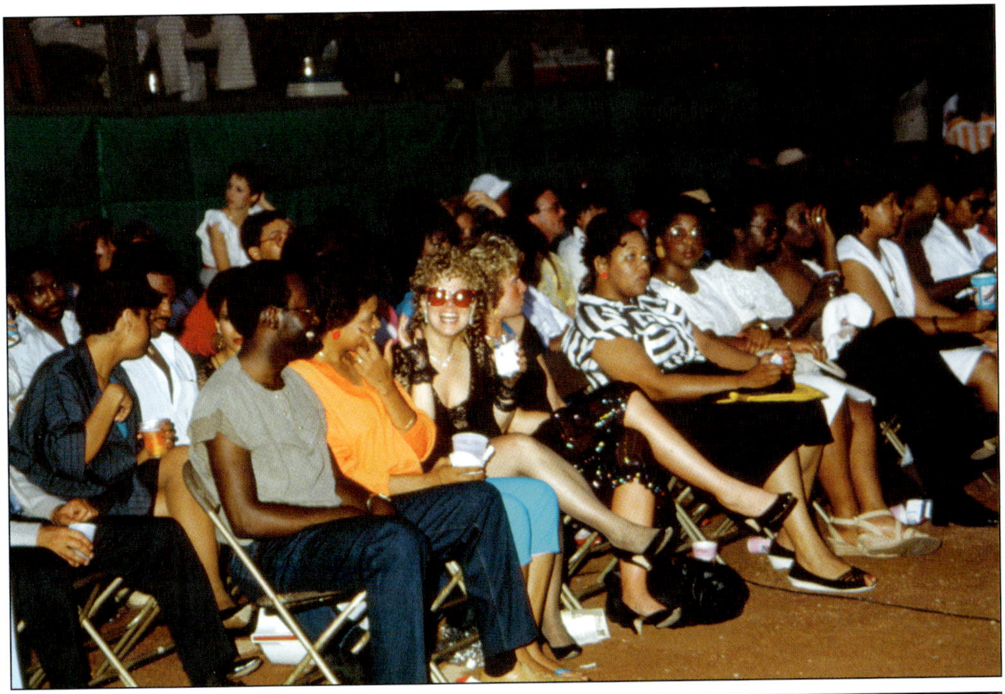

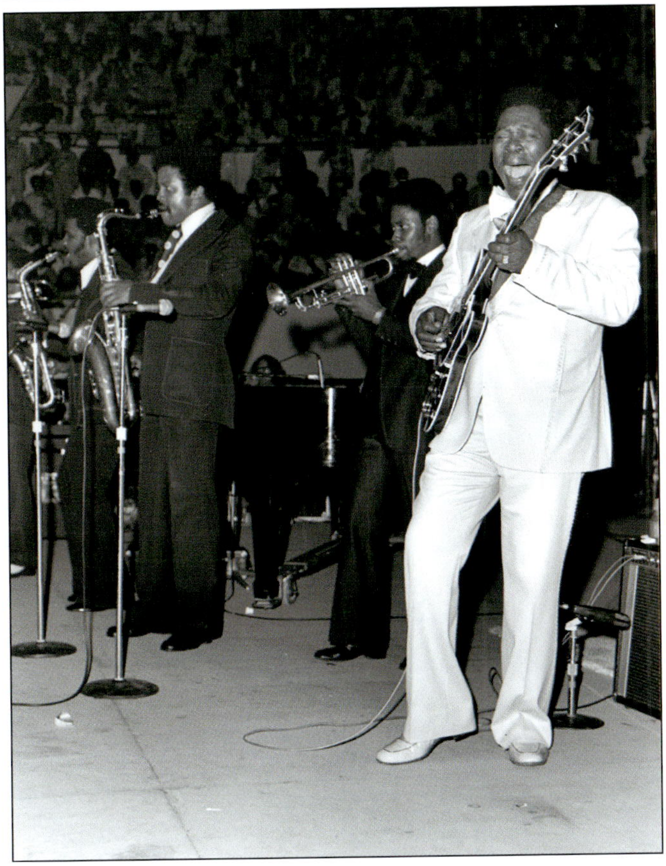

To be among the first nonsporting events permitted in the new stadium was a recognition of the festival's acceptance by Cincinnati as a whole and a benchmark moment for its local promoter. Dino Santangelo stated to the *Cincinnati Enquirer*: "The proudest thing was the ease with which a contract was negotiated with Riverfront Stadium, in other words, I feel that marks the highlight of 10 years. If we can, on our end live up to an obligation to present a good Festival within the stadium, stage it right, do it correctly, then the Festival will be around for another 10 years . . . I want our 10th Anniversary Ohio Valley Jazz Festival to be the most exciting yet. I want the city to be proud of this Festival." B.B. King and his guitar, Lucille (right), stole the show on Saturday night.

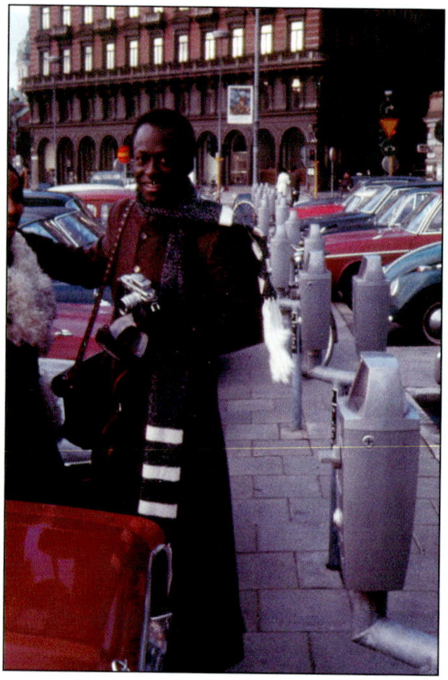

In addition to his many other festival-related duties between 1970 and 1974, Santangelo travelled across Europe as tour manager for Count Basie, Dave Brubeck, Charles Mingus, and Miles Davis (at left and below). Davis later noted that "Dino was one of the few white men that I liked." Their friendship extended beyond Europe, where Santangelo's legendary ability to make "molehills out of mountains" smoothed the way for the jazz players he shepherded. Davis got to know Santangelo well—in particular, his weakness for fine dining. While traveling in Morocco, Davis called to report that his hotel had wonderful French food and that Santangelo should get on a plane and join him.

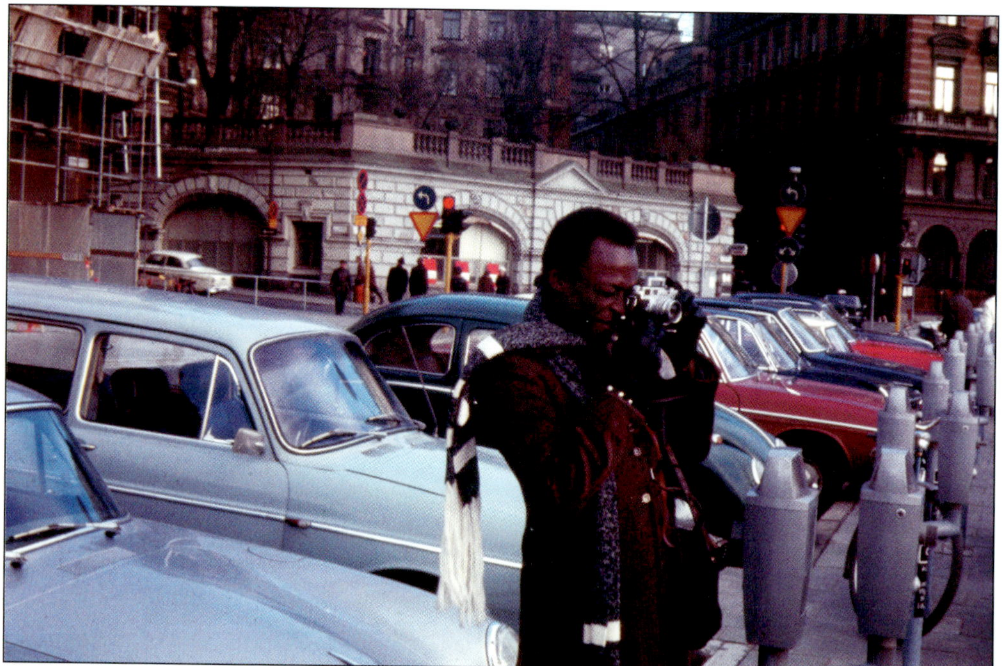

Touring with a group of jazz musicians is a challenge anywhere and at any time, but in the 1970s, Europe was at the front line of the Cold War, requiring diplomacy to navigate. The Berlin Wall had been built in 1961, requiring anyone passing between East and West Germany to use official checkpoints. One of these, known to the world as "Checkpoint Charlie," had been the site of several tragic attempts by refugees to flee East Germany. Santangelo once helped bypass a customs check that would have incriminated one of the musicians by discretely moving a particular bag to the "checked" pile.

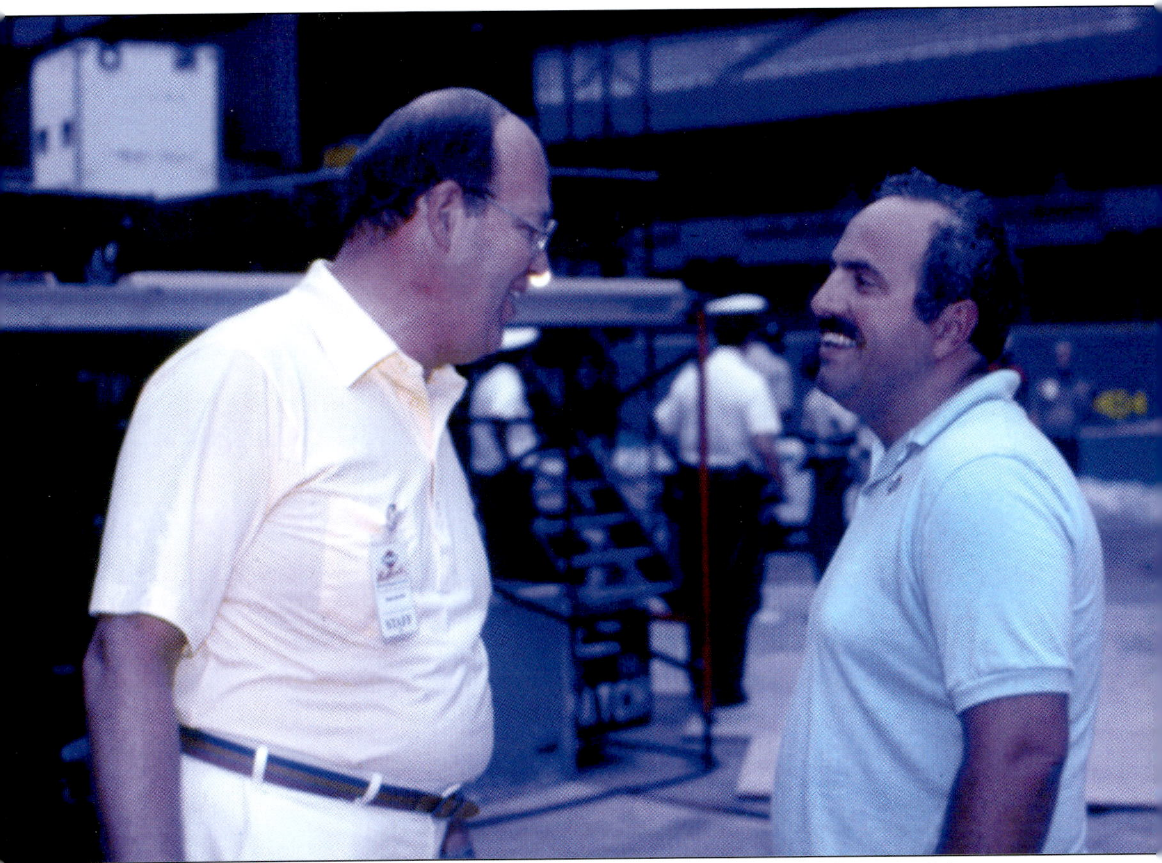

Family and friends play prominent roles in producing the festivals. Dino Santangelo's youngest brother, Joe (right), gave the national festivals a solid financial foundation, coordinated the bookkeeping for multiple tours, and simultaneously managed box office operations for all of the agency's ventures. With Dino's untimely death in 1986, Joe continued to produce the Cincinnati festival, now held at Paul Brown Stadium. Dino's childhood friend Chuck Hertlein (left) handled festival concessions, or "merch." Programs, cups, and T-shirts were standard concert fare, but many other items were produced in connection with the national tours, especially during the Kool years. Imported maracas were popular (though they were often hard to get in sufficient quantities), as were programs, playing cards, buttons, key holders, glow sticks, and many other specialty items.

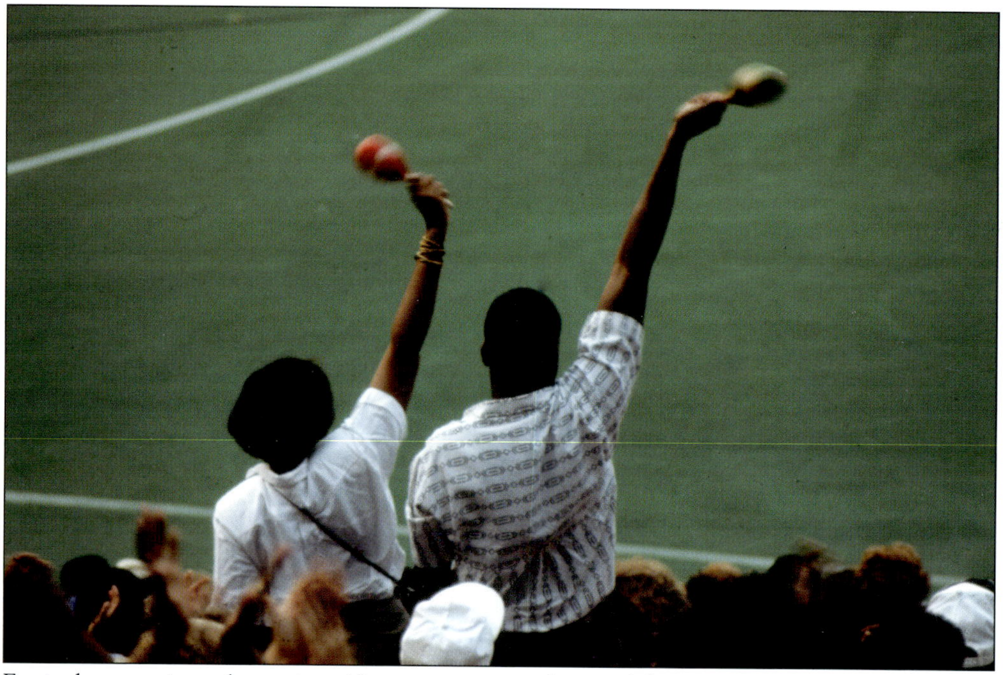

Festival concession sales nationwide were an integral part of the event's promotion and carried a sponsor's logo to cities across the country. Like the festival's stage, concessions traveled from market to market, coordinating sales with the venues at which the events were held. Note the popular maracas above. Scott Santangelo (below, left) and Brad Krassner (below, right) were part of the festival's national concessions team.

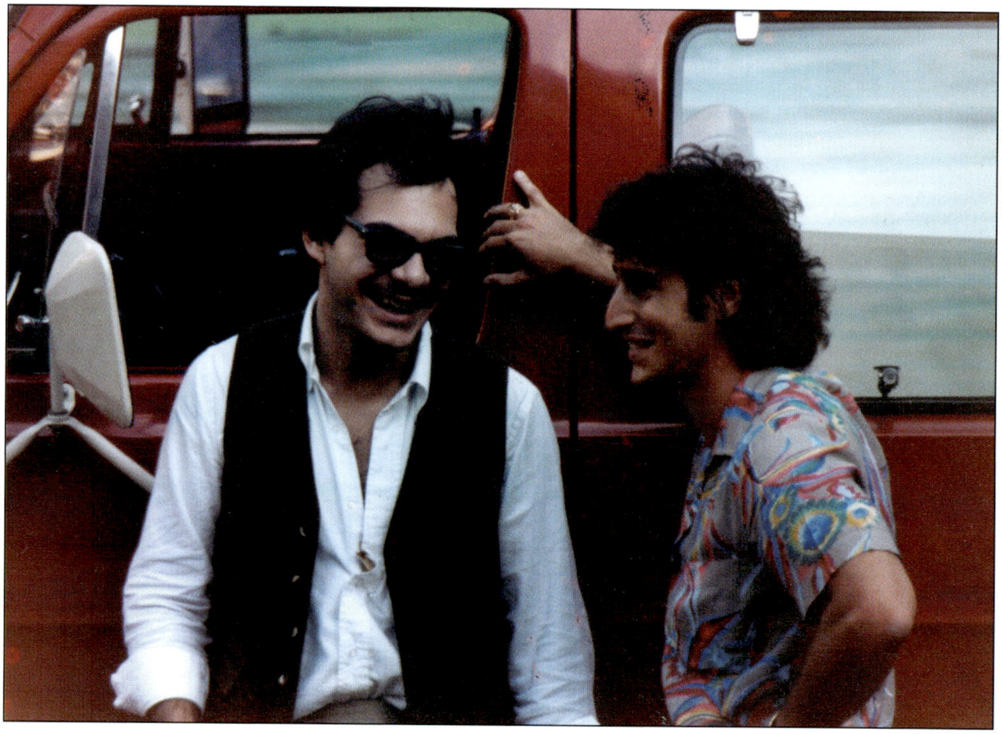

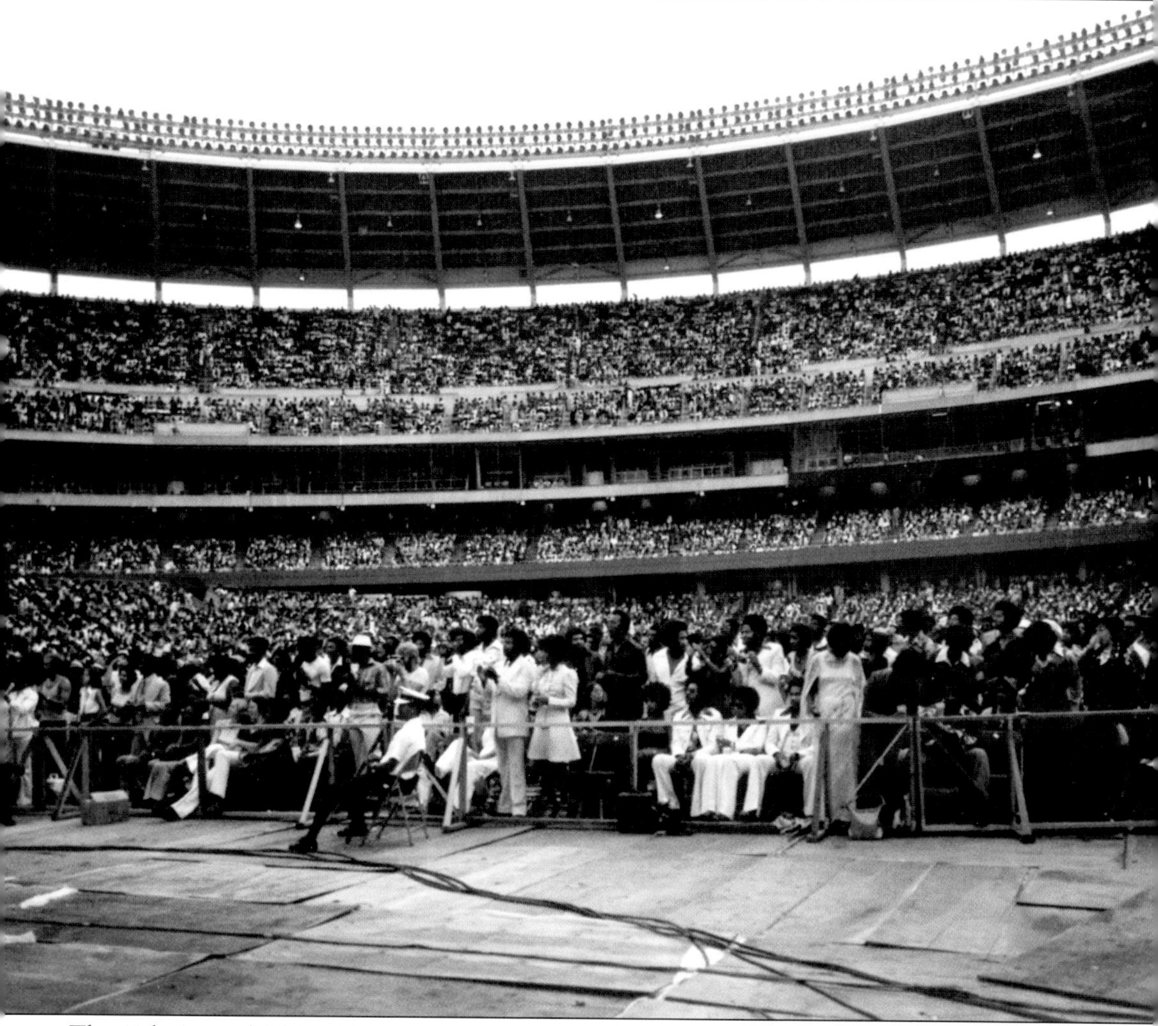

The 11th Annual Ohio Valley Jazz Festival was held at Riverfront Stadium in 1972. The 1970s saw traditional jazz acts slowly yield to more mainstream talent. The show on Friday, July 21 featured the Jimmy Smith Jam Session (with Kenny Burrell, Jimmy Owens, Joe Newman, Roy Haynes, Zoot Sims, and Illinois Jacquet), Les McCann, Ray Charles, B.B. King, and the Ike & Tina Turner Revue. Ike and Tina Turner were a challenge on a show with multiple performers. Dino Santangelo and George Wein telegrammed their agent, reminding him of the "disruption of production of our shows at prior Festivals, caused by late arrival of equipment and band." The Saturday performance on July 22 included the Thad Jones/Mel Lewis Orchestra, Cannonball Adderley, Nina Simone, the Giants of Jazz (with Thelonious Monk, Dizzy Gillespie, Sonny Stitt, Art Blakey, Kai Winding, and Al McKibbon), and Lou Rawls.

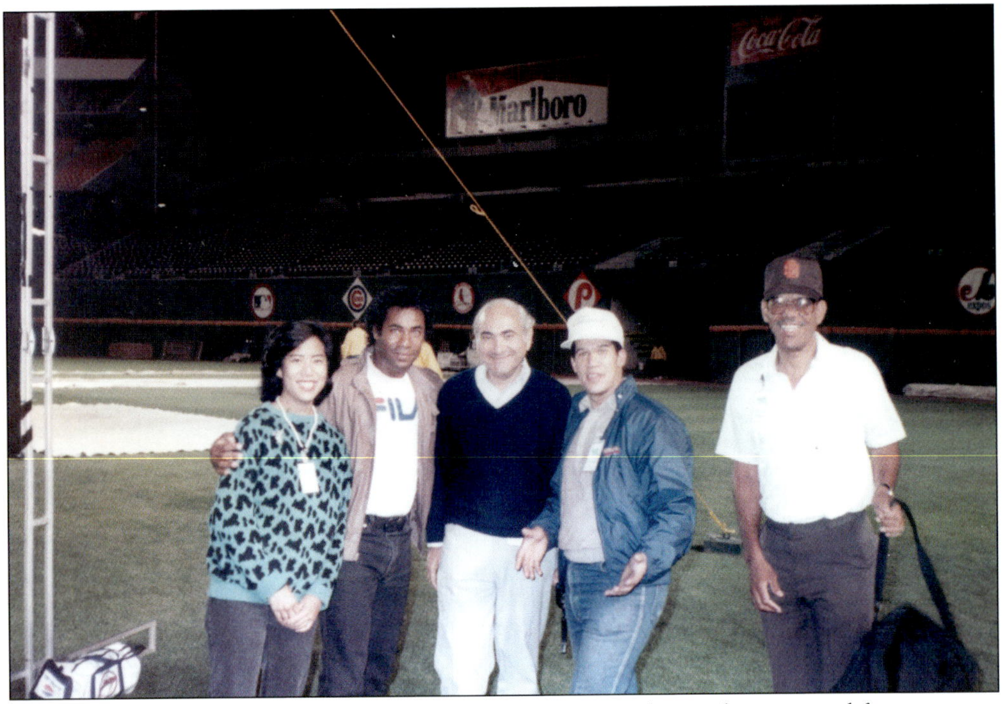

The jazz festival in Cincinnati had become part of a national tour that spanned from coast to coast. Oakland, California, was a strong festival market, and Darlene Chan led the local staff of Festival Productions, Inc. This photograph shows, from left to right, Chan, Caesar Churchwell, Dino Santangelo, stage manager Jim Garvey, and festival security director Rick Rhodes.

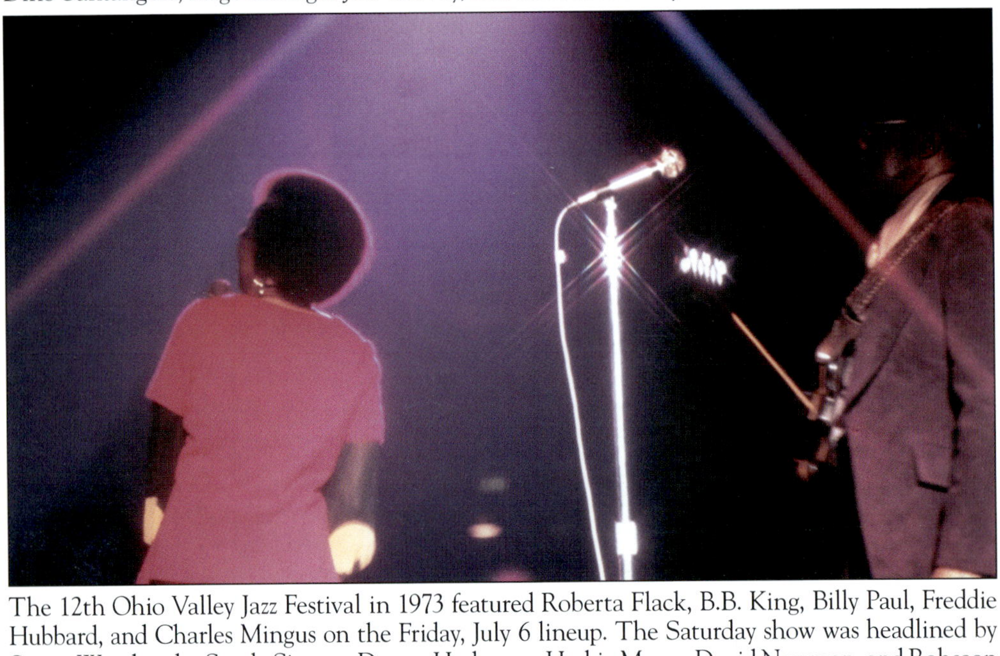

The 12th Ohio Valley Jazz Festival in 1973 featured Roberta Flack, B.B. King, Billy Paul, Freddie Hubbard, and Charles Mingus on the Friday, July 6 lineup. The Saturday show was headlined by Stevie Wonder, the Staple Singers, Donny Hathaway, Herbie Mann, David Newman, and Rahsaan Roland Kirk. The city's first African American mayor, Ted Berry, proclaimed Ohio Valley Jazz Festival Week in Cincinnati. Mavis and "Pops" Staples of the Staple Singers are pictured above.

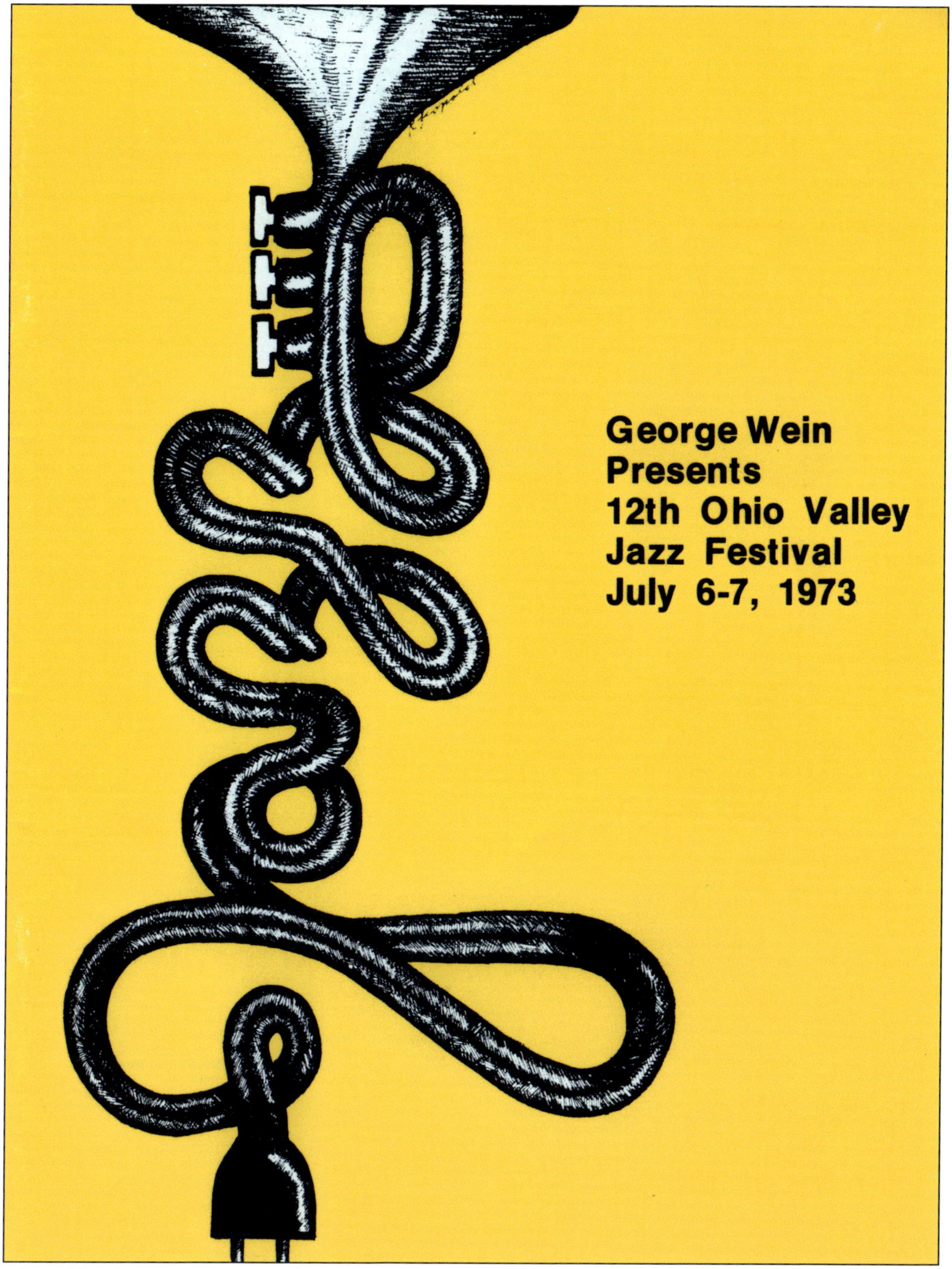

The official program from 1973 trumpeted a jazz-themed logo. But as the events grew larger, lineups featured fewer jazz acts. A midnight dance at Music Hall's Topper Club that year would feature the Duke Ellington Orchestra.

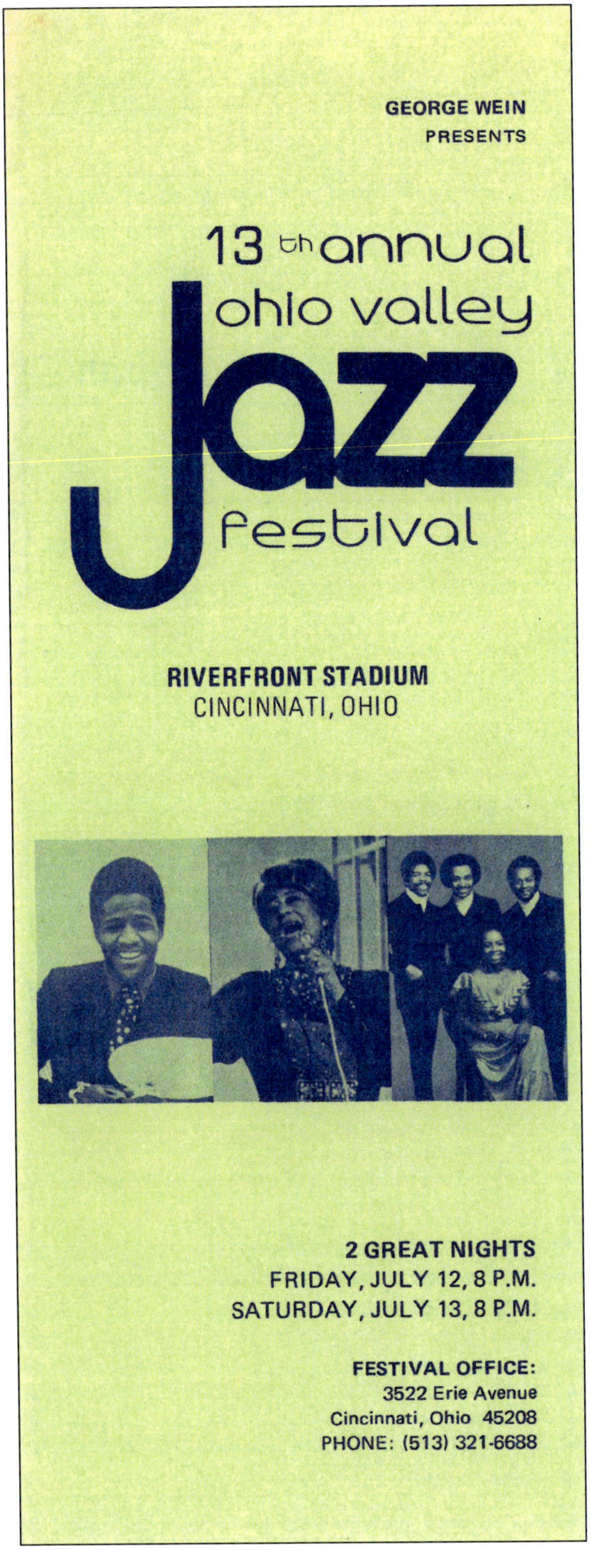

The 13th Ohio Valley Jazz Festival kicked off on Friday, July 12, 1974, with Gladys Knight & the Pips, the O'Jays, Herbie Hancock, Tower of Power, and Donald Byrd. Saturday featured Al Green, Ella Fitzgerald, the Crusaders, Return to Forever, and the Jimmy Smith Trio with Gene Ammons. The festival office was often an advocate for its patrons in disputes with local establishments over services. As the festival increasingly appealed to an African American audience, there was a deeper concern that many of these disputes were racially motivated. In response to one complaint, Santangelo wrote Holiday Inns of America: "I am shocked at the treatment [the patrons] received at your hotel . . . Since we plan to repeat the same Festival next year, we would very much like to know in advance whether this situation was an isolated incident that never should have happened, or whether our patrons, be they white, black, yellow, green, or orange, can expect better treatment from Holiday Inns in the future." The expanding tour schedule, combined with the regional draw of each event, gave the festivals increasing leverage to represent its ticket buyers on such issues.

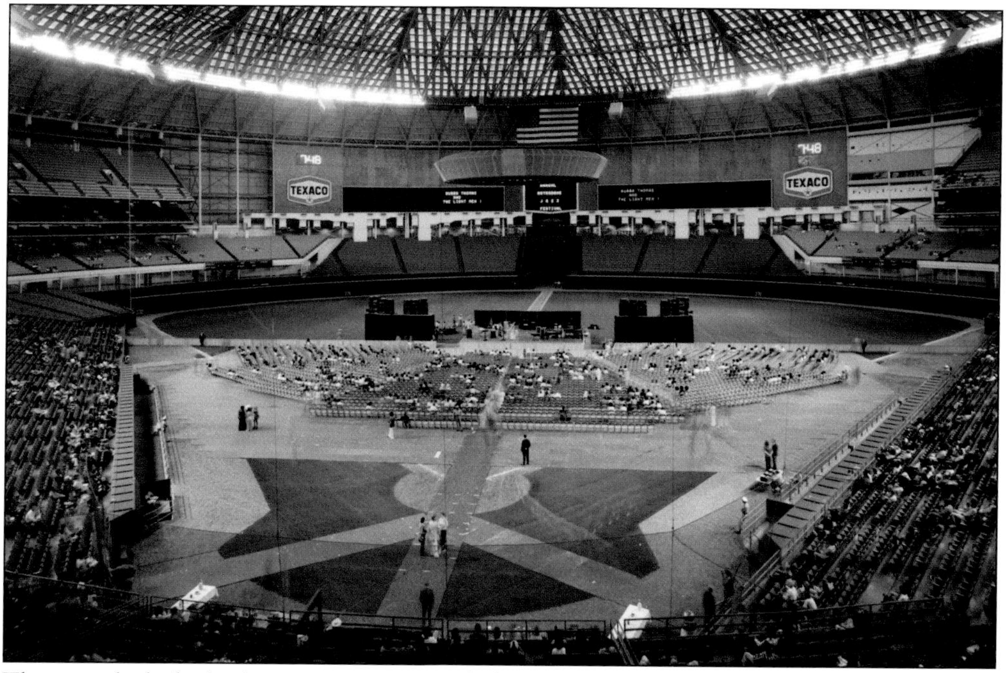

There was little doubt that patrons were satisfied with the caliber of the entertainment. One note mailed to the festival offices in Cincinnati read, "Gentlemen: I would like to congratulate all who was responsible for that super-bad jazz festival in 73, it was together. A person could really get in to it . . . Out of sight . . . And that close up screen was just right . . . So keep up the good work . . . And I know this year 74 will be just as together as last year's show . . . Right-on, a jazz fan. Thanks." In Houston, Texas, the festival was held at the newly constructed Astrodome (above).

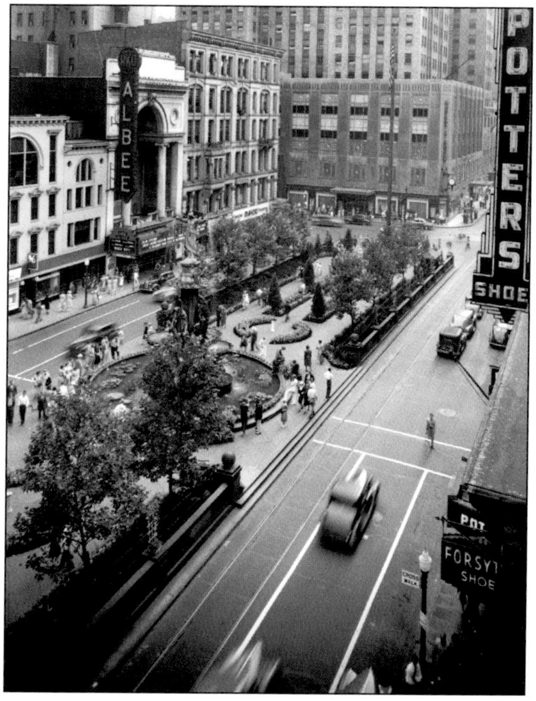

In 1974, Dino Santangelo was busy at home producing a concert with Miles Davis at Music Hall and making an effort to save the historic Albee Theater, jeopardized by the rapid development of Cincinnati's downtown core. Santangelo offered to manage the Albee and guarantee rentals, but it was not to be. The theater gave way to a major real estate development that saw the removal of the historic Fountain esplanade and the relocation of the iconic Tyler-Davidson Fountain. In Atlanta that year, headliner Aretha Franklin failed to appear at the jazz festival, and Harold Melvin and the Blue Notes were an overnight substitute. Atlanta's first black mayor, Maynard Jackson, had the audience hold up their lighters in support of Franklin's family emergency.

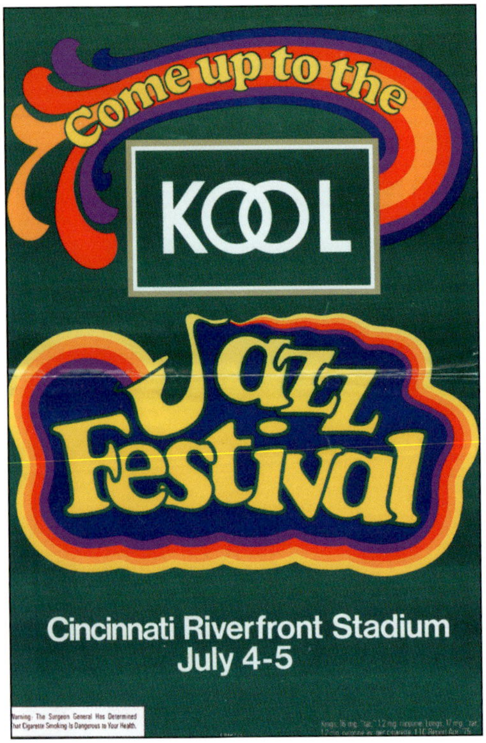

The 1975 festival was the 14th in Cincinnati and the first year of sponsorship by Kool cigarettes. On Friday, July 4, Riverfront Stadium hosted the O'Jays, the Isley Brothers, Harold Melvin & the Blue Notes, Ramsey Lewis, Freddie Hubbard, and Gato Barbieri. Saturday's show included the Ohio Players, the Staple Singers, the Stylistics, B.B. King, McCoy Tyner, and Bobbi Humphrey. In Houston, Texas, that year, Santangelo was recognized by the mayor for the Astrodome Jazz Festival's contribution to black culture in the Houston community. The festival had truly become a national program. The Cincinnati staff that year included, from left to right, Bob Jones, Joe Santangelo, Nancy Bick Clark, Willie Price, Dino Santangelo, Rose Kohake, John Sdoucas, and Fedora Volpe.

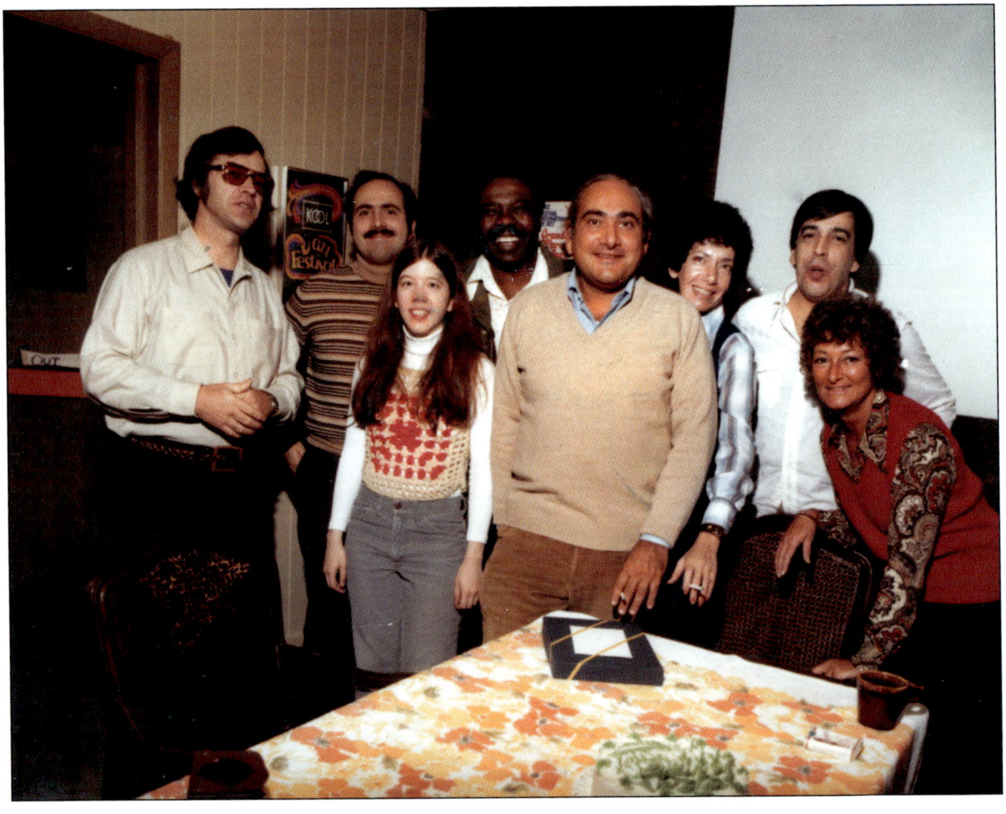

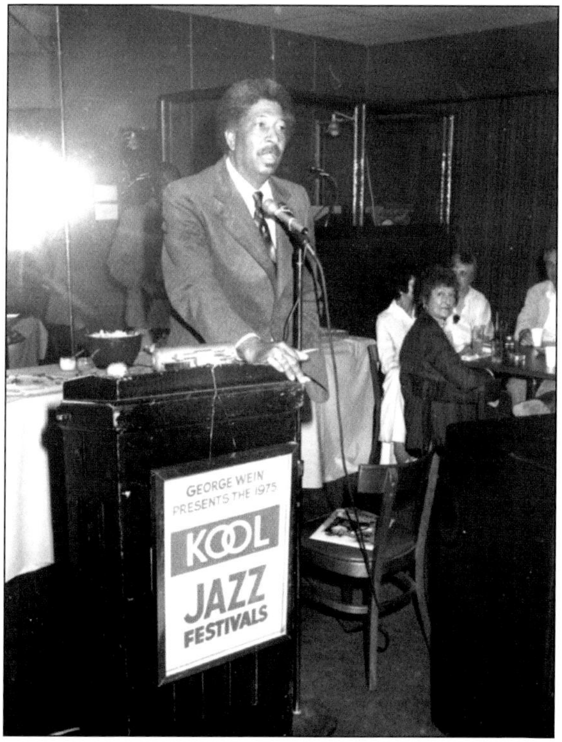

The festivals relied heavily on local support in each city on the tour. Key liaisons were often colorful personalities, well known in their communities. In Texas, Skipper Lee Frazier (right) coordinated local media, promotions, hotels, and much more. The festival's Cincinnati staff were always welcome guests in town. The photograph below shows, from left to right, Willie Price, Brad Broecker, an unidentified sponsor representative, Jan and Dino Santangelo, two unidentified local representatives, Skipper Lee Frazier, and Nancy Bick Clark.

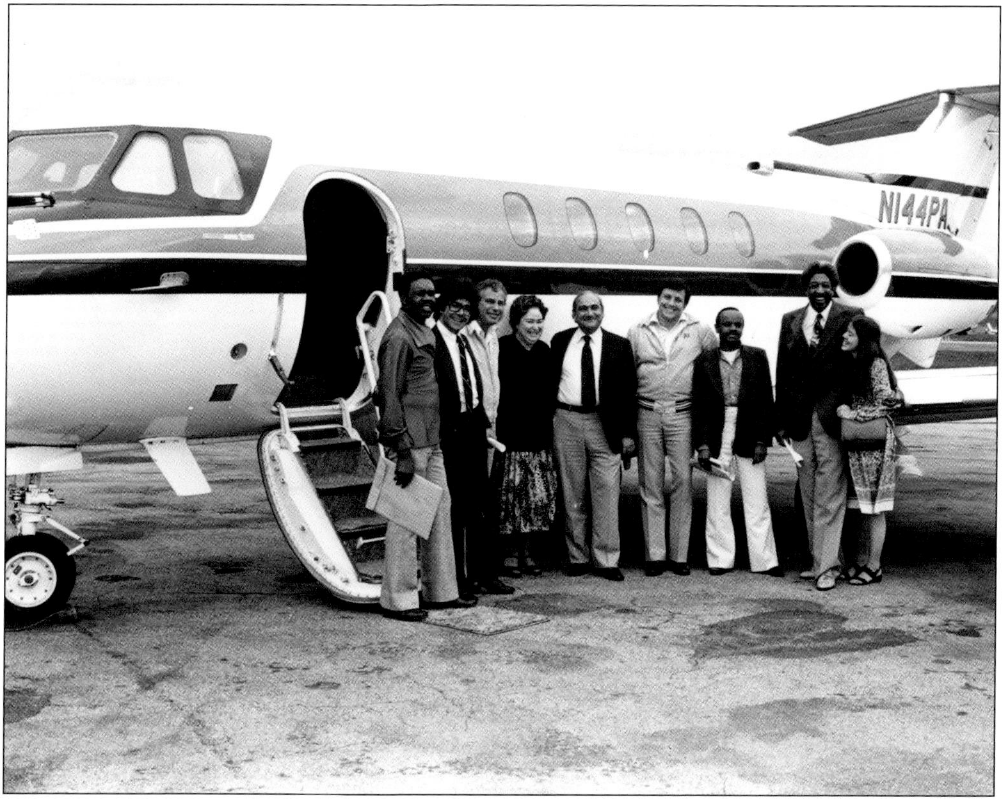

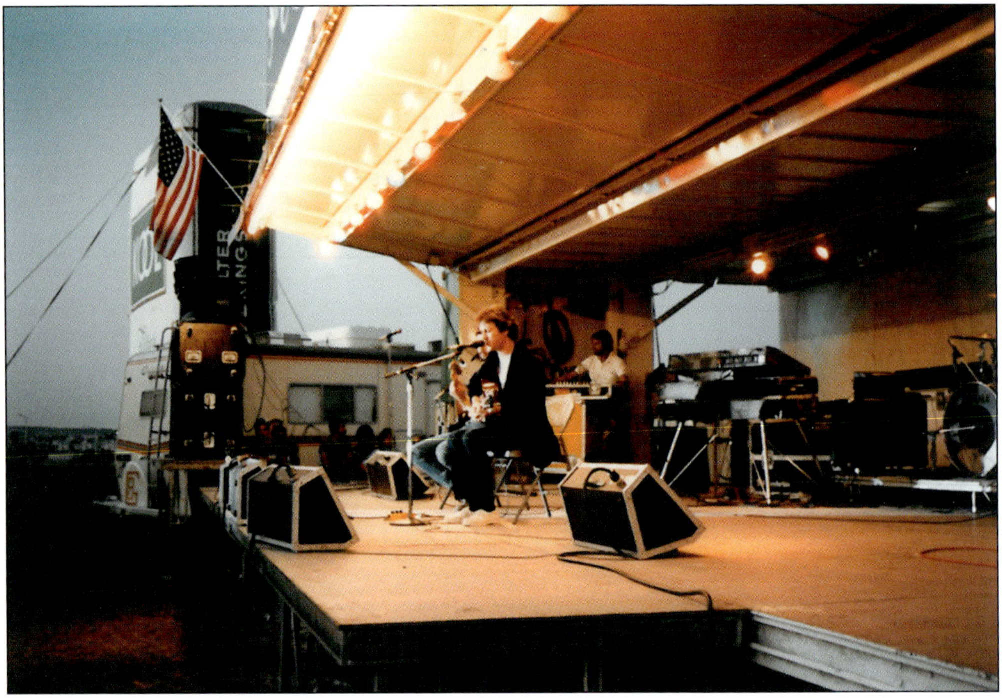

The sponsorship of Kool cigarettes represented a major shift in the marketing of the festivals and led to a major expansion of advertising and promotional efforts in support of the events. It also enabled an expansion in the number and type of events, which grew to include clubs, theaters, military bases, and free concerts. In the heyday of the Kool years, the festival became just one of many different programs held nationwide and the headlining acts part of touring lineups appearing at multiple events.

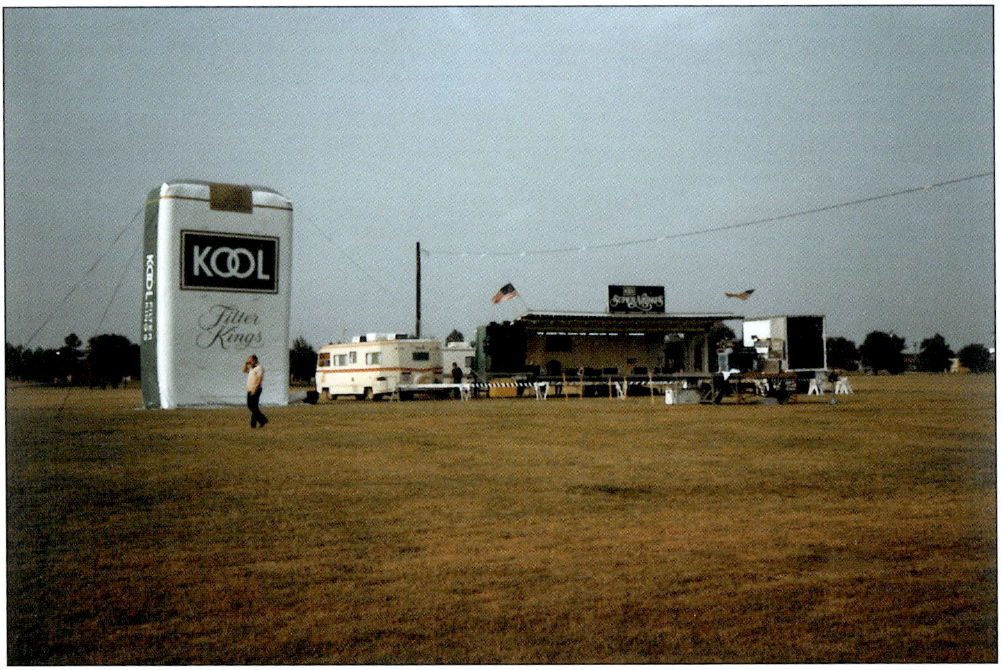

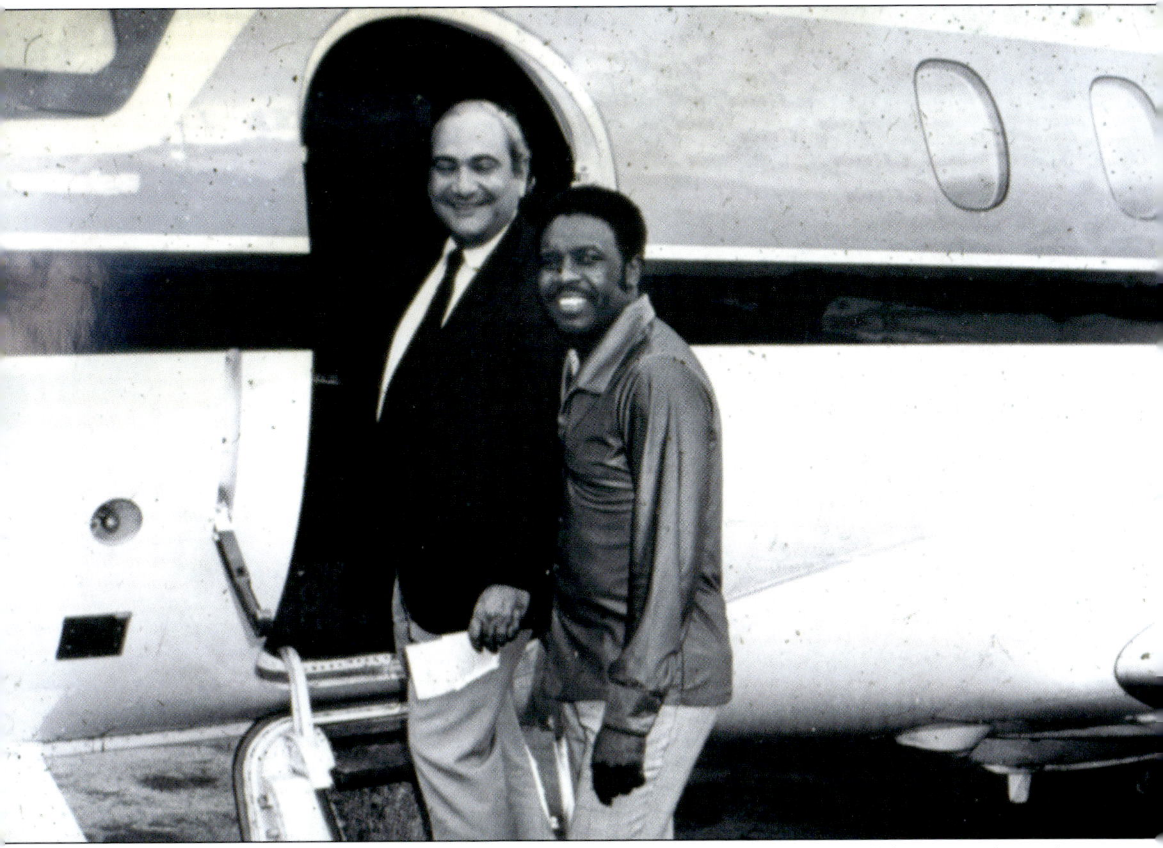

Dino Santangelo and his Cincinnati staff travelled extensively in support of the many festivals being produced across the country. The photograph above shows Santangelo (left) and Willie Price (right) catching a flight between cities, a frequent necessity across the national tour. The personal touch paid dividends, and local staff were engaged throughout the year in preparation for the festival's annual return.

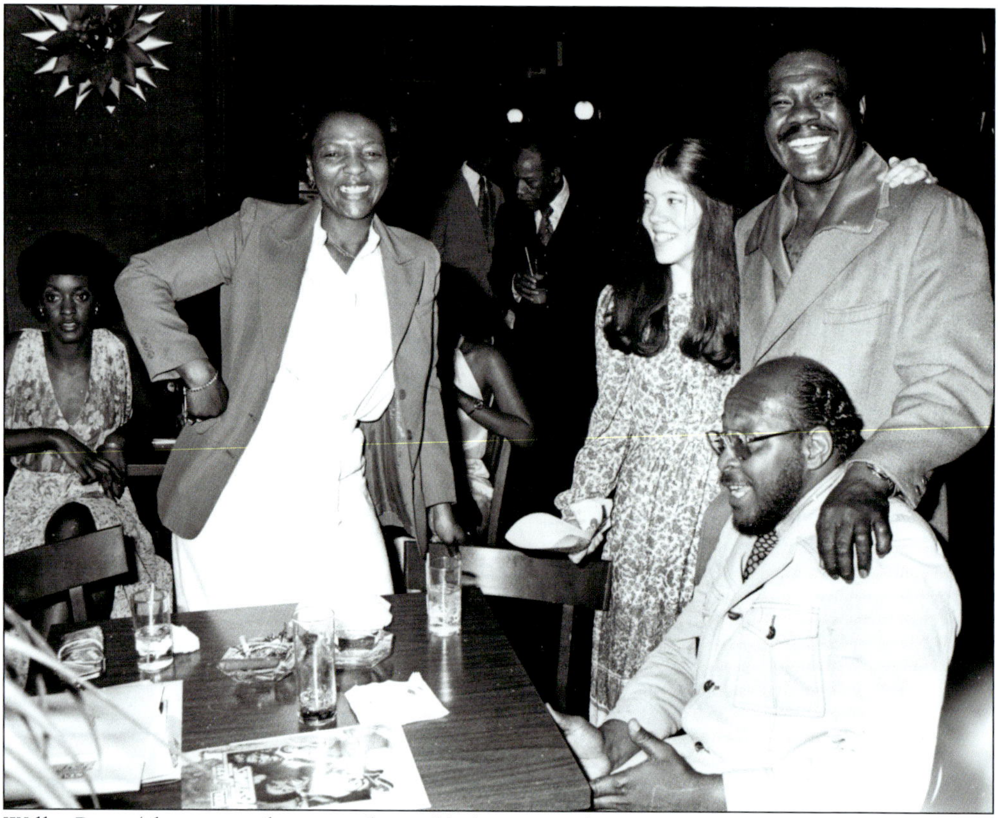

Willie Price (above, standing at right and below, center) was officially the festival's tour group coordinator. As the festivals expanded so did his reputation as a ladies' man and liaison between tour groups, the festival, and the many third parties involved in the annual pilgrimage to the event (notably hotels, transportation, and after parties). Colorful, loyal, and personable, Price made the festival offices a lively place to work, and his overheard phone conversations were the topic of even livelier discussion.

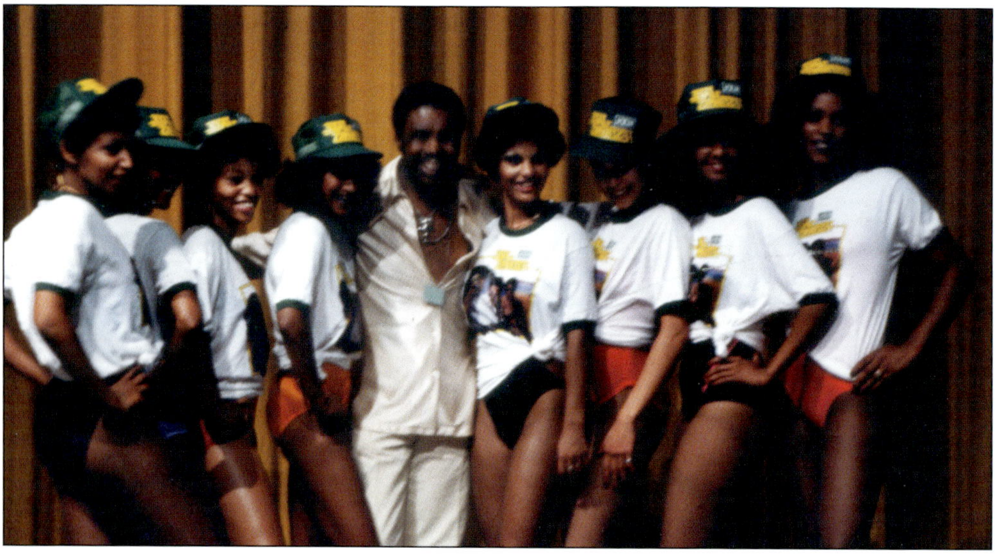

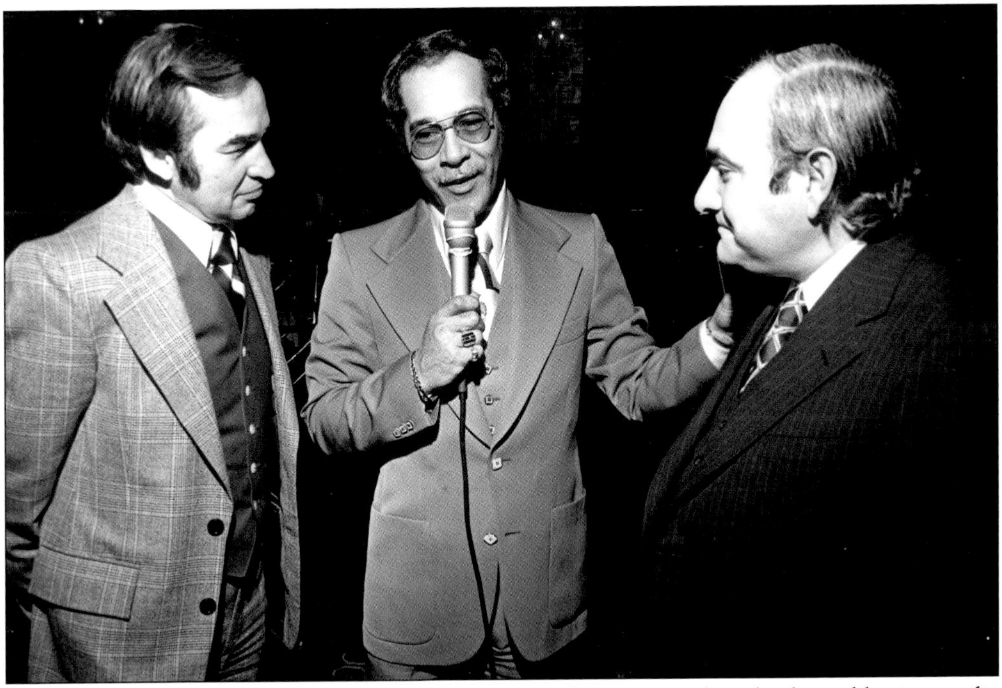

Santangelo had significant home court advantages in Cincinnati, where he formed lasting media partnerships. In the photograph above, Santangelo (far right) is seen with Sonny Burns (center), VP/GM of legendary Cincinnati radio station WCIN, and an unidentified man (left). In the image below, Fred Suggs (second from left) and Santangelo (second from right) lineup for a press photograph. Suggs was the owner/publisher of Cincinnati's popular *NIP* magazine. In addition to its paid advertising, the festival donated tickets to the city's recreation department and made direct grants to local charities, generating a goodwill that could not otherwise be purchased. Groups who received tickets expressed their gratitude in many ways. The City Workhouse noted, "We have nothing to offer in return, except perhaps a bed and 3 squares a day if you ever need it, and certainly our appreciation."

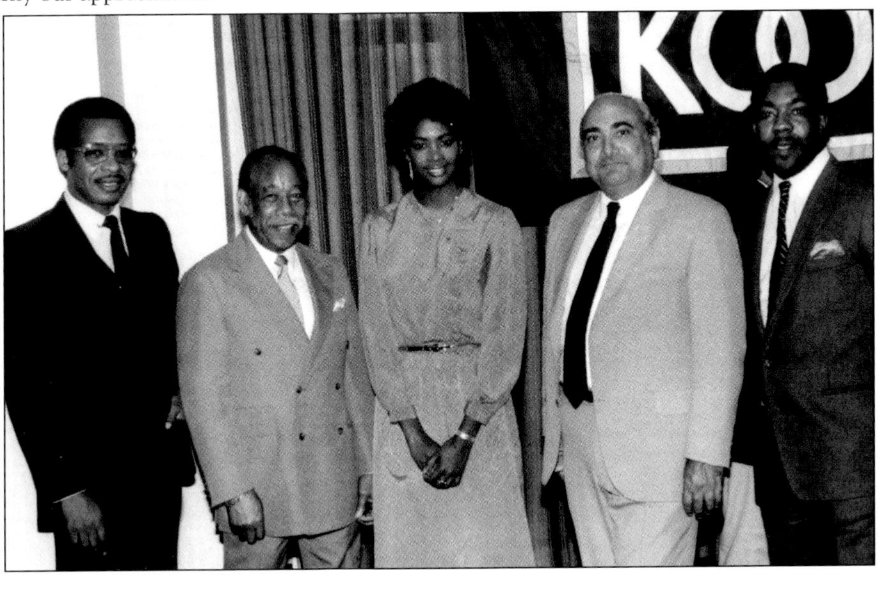

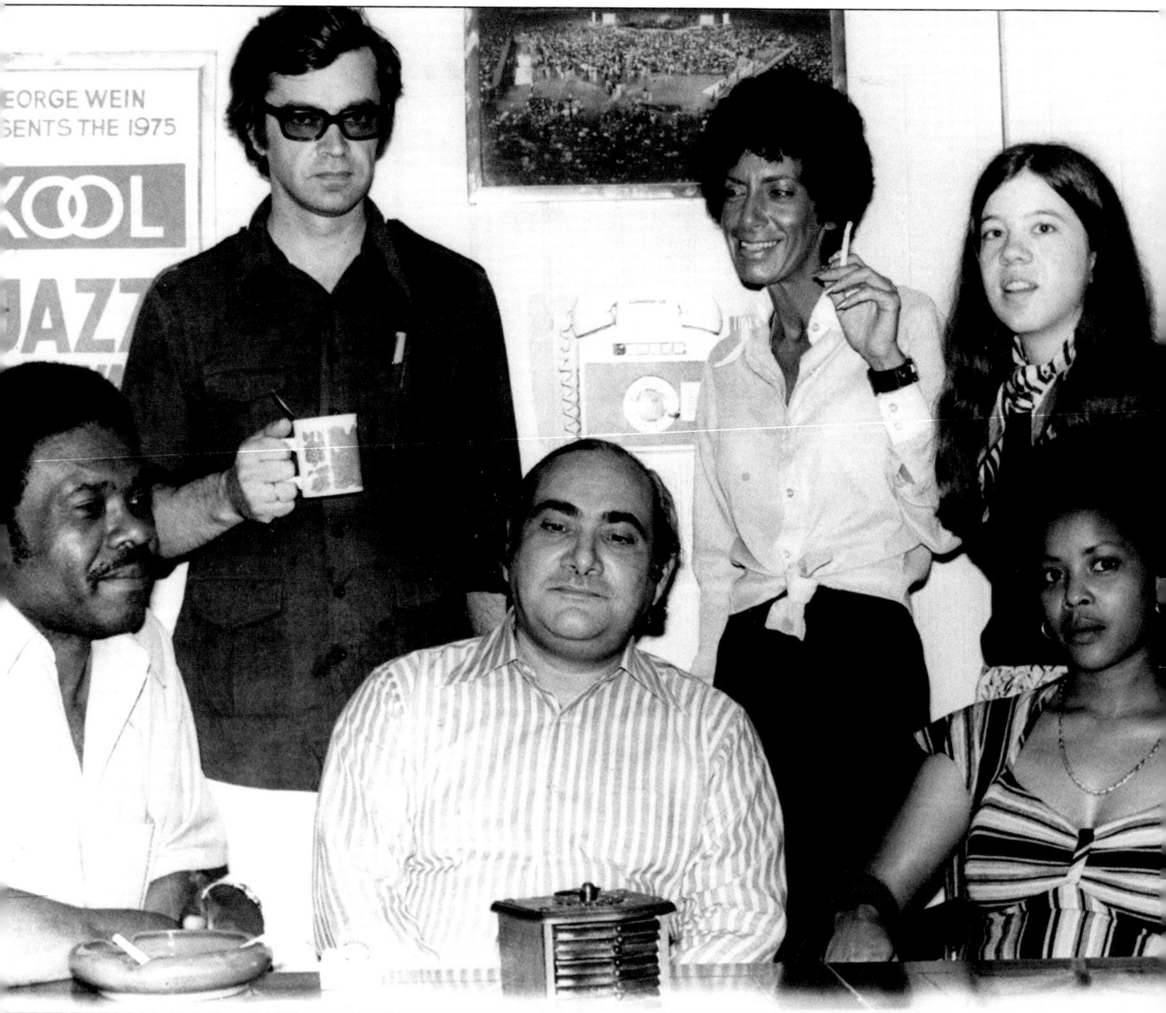

Part of the 1975 festival staff at the Cincinnati office included, from left to right, Willie Price, Bob Jones, Dino Santangelo, Rose Kohake, Nancy Bick Clark, and an unidentified office staffer (seated). Notably absent in the photograph are Joe Santangelo (Dino's brother) and Fedora Volpe (Dino's executive secretary).

Five

1976–1980

The Kool Years

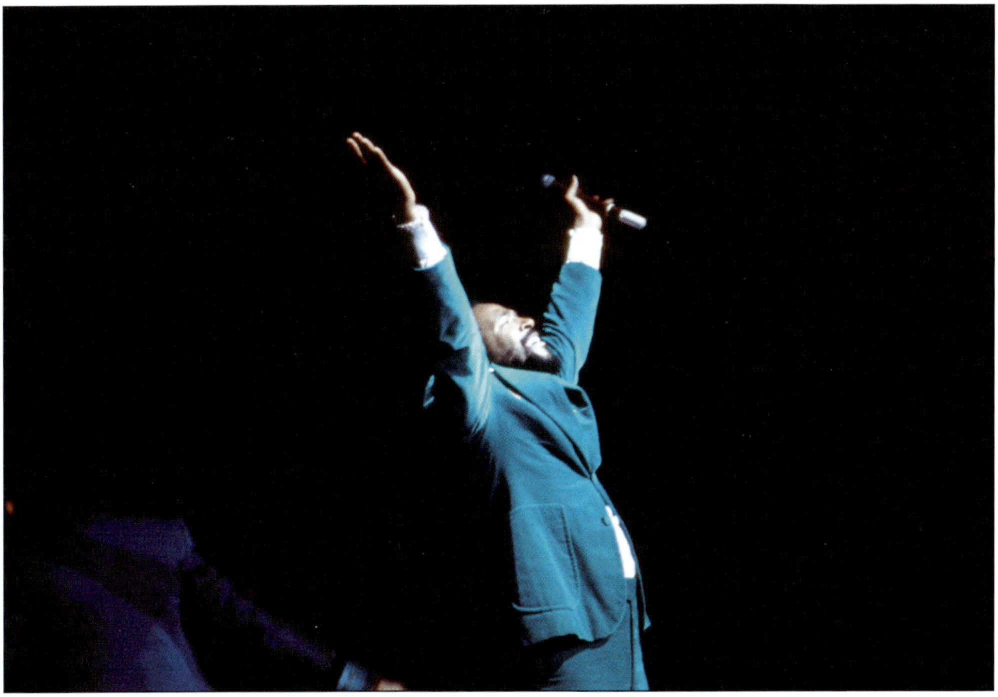

The 1976 concert was the 15th festival held at Riverfront Stadium. Performers on Friday, July 23 included Marvin Gaye (above), the Temptations, Nancy Wilson, and Archie Bell & the Drells. Saturday night featured the Spinners, Natalie Cole, Harold Melvin & the Blue Notes, the Chi Lites, B.B. King, and Roy Ayers Ubiquity.

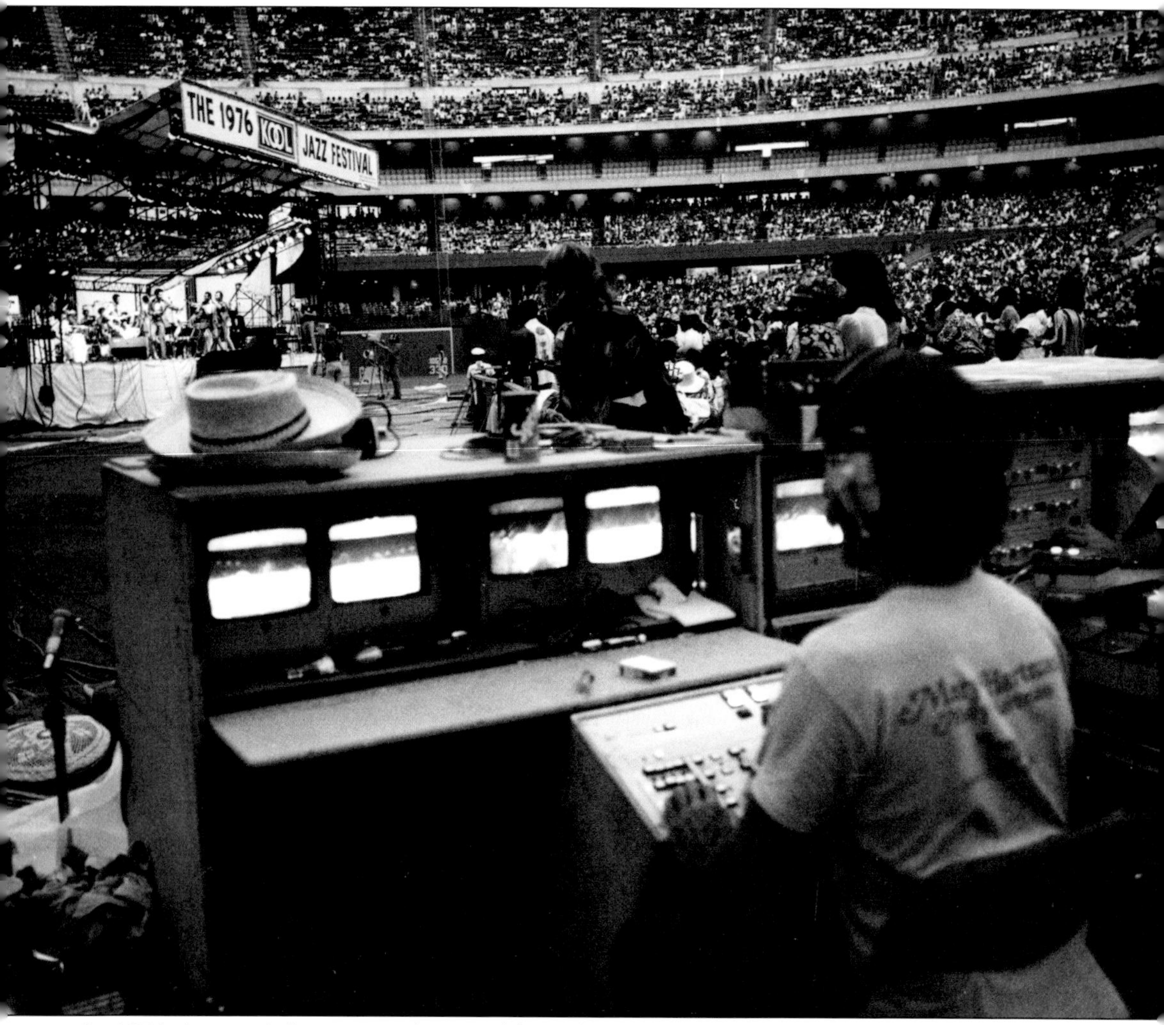

In 1976, America's bicentennial was celebrated, and that year would also see the Cincinnati Reds win their second consecutive World Series in October. The Kool Jazz Festival in July, with its extensive field setups and seating, was a testament to the solid working relationship between Dino Santangelo and the city departments that managed Riverfront Stadium. The festival had been the venue's first nonsporting event in 1970 and remained an annual feature on the calendar until the stadium's demolition in 2002.

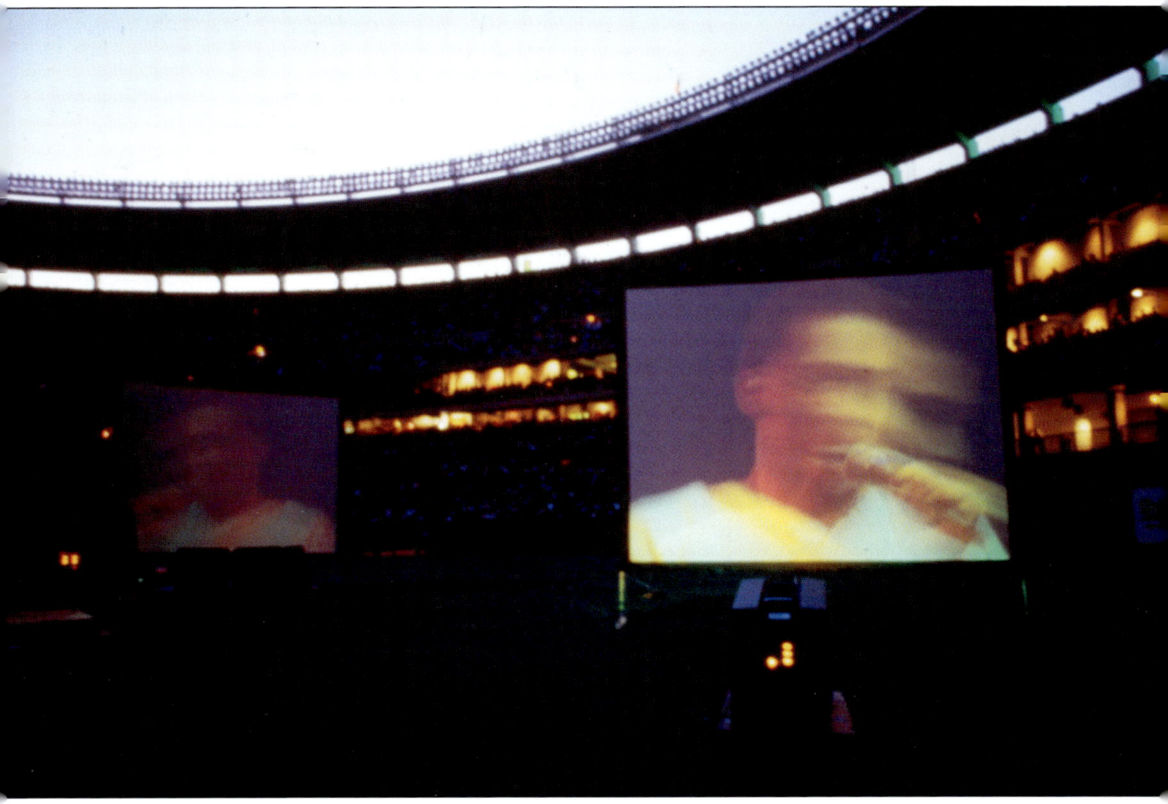

The 1977 festival featured new innovations: the festival's popular closed-circuit television was in color and each night included an exciting laser light show. Patrons from coast to coast could also charge tickets by phone, coordinated through the Cincinnati office. Artists appearing on Friday, June 23 included George Benson, the O'Jays, LTD, Al Jarreau, and George Duke. Saturday's show included Gladys Knight & the Pips, Ashford & Simpson, Grover Washington Jr. & Locksmith, Brick, and the Duke Ellington Orchestra (conducted by Mercer Ellington). Following that year's event in Chicago, Dino Santangelo received a thank-you note from an emerging figure on the political stage, the Reverend Jesse Jackson: "Dear Dino, On behalf of Operation PUSH, I would like to extend my warm and sincere appreciation to you for providing me the opportunity to address the Kool Jazz Festival audience. I must tell you how impressed I was by your organization. It was a demonstration of the pursuit of a common goal, resulting in a smooth running, orderly and successful event . . . Dino, you have the knowledge, know-how, a competent organization, and the talent to make any concert endeavor a success."

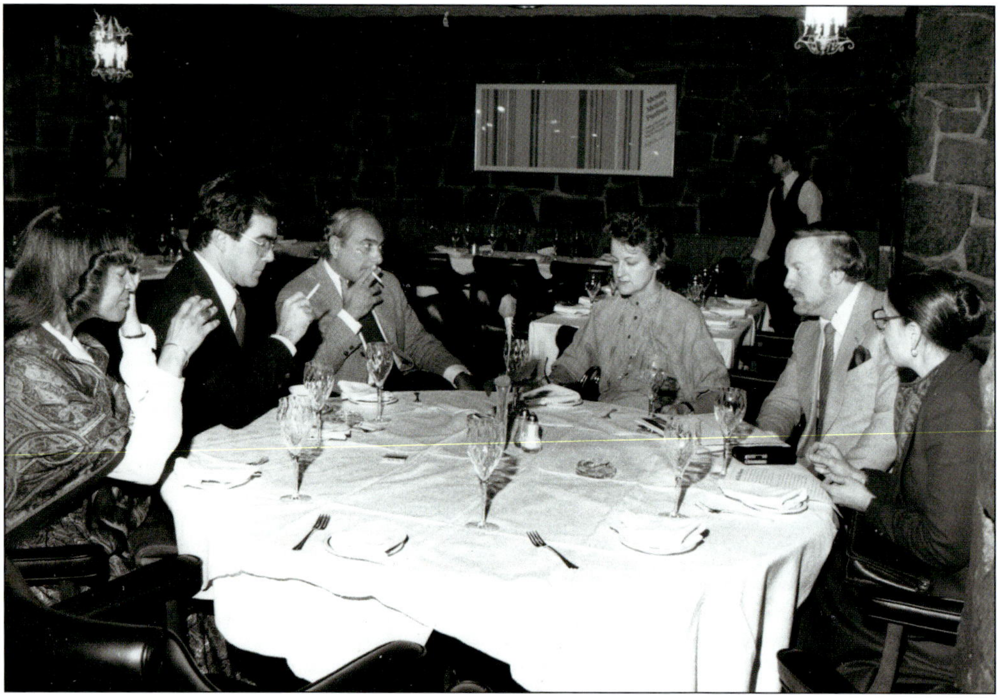

Along with Kool's sponsorship came the obligation to coordinate with that company's many representatives. There would be numerous meetings with Kool festival staff; in this photograph are, from left to right, Marie St. Louis (from the festival's New York office), Brad Broecker (Kool), Dino Santangelo, Virginia Thompson and Frank McKeown (Kool), and Nancy Bick Clark (from the festival's Cincinnati office).

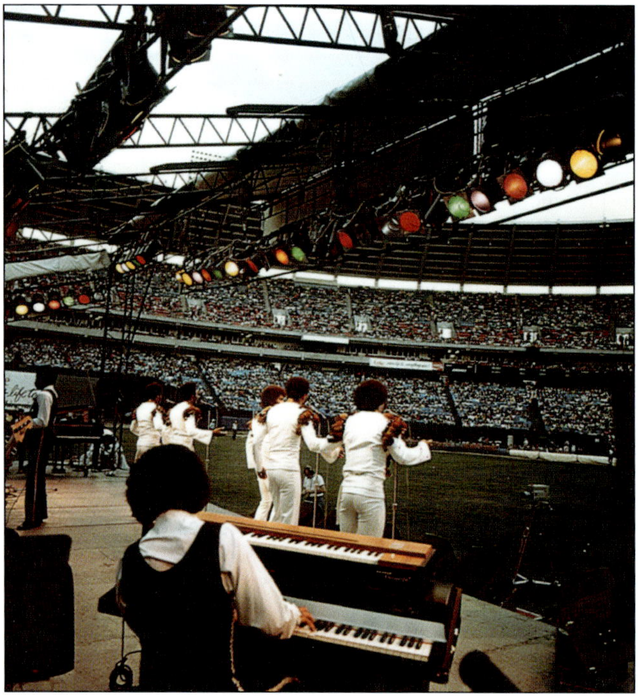

The festivals were incredibly popular events, and Kool's advertising and promotional support enabled them to maintain a high profile in the markets that hosted them. They were also prestigious events at which to perform, and entertainers and their booking agents jockeyed for position on the lineups. Beyond the fees they were paid, artists benefitted through their appearances and the related publicity, which boosted awareness of their latest material and directly impacted record sales.

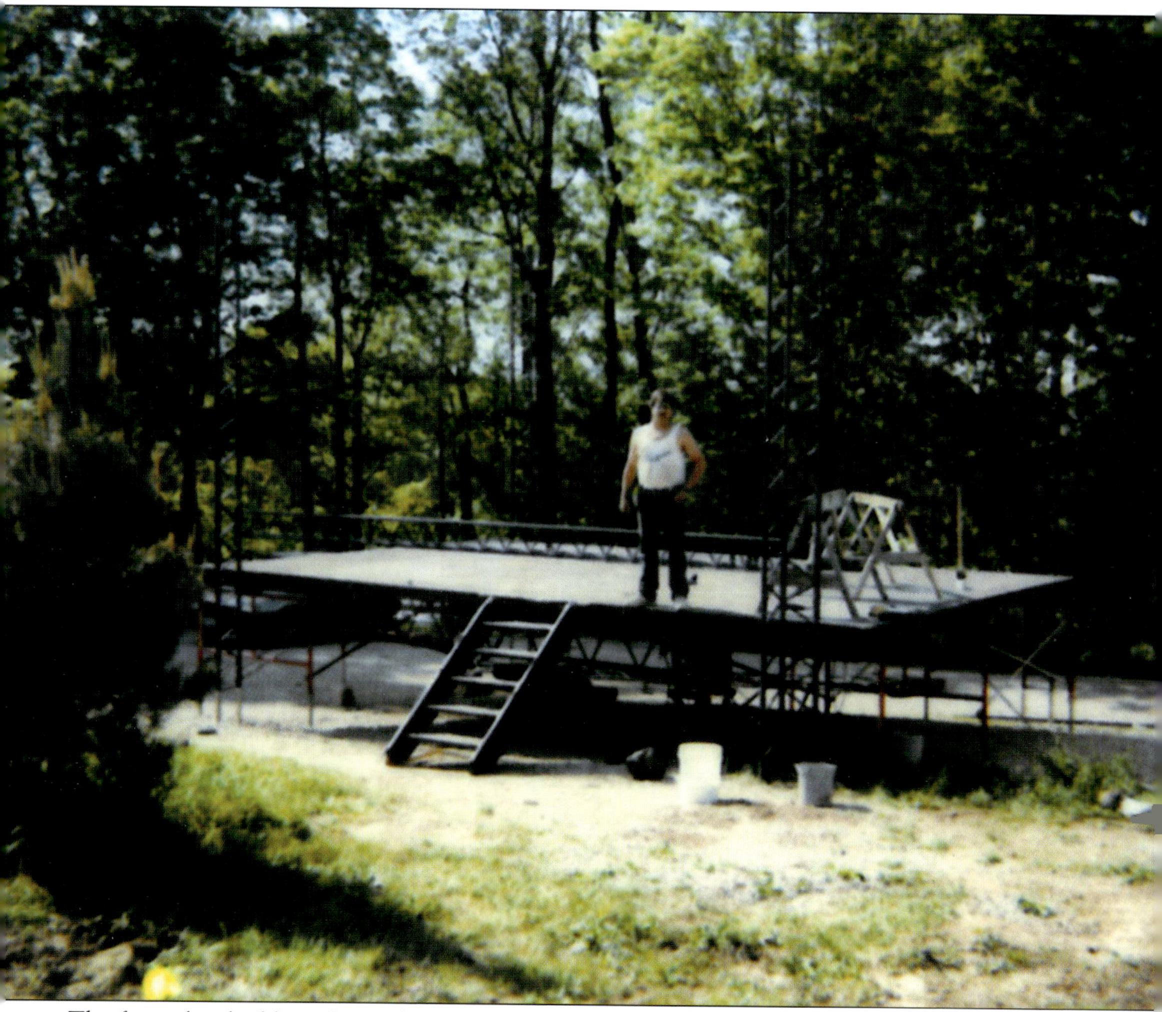

The festivals relied heavily on the support of vendors for technical production. From field prep to stage, sound, lighting, and video packages, there were countless challenges associated with presenting events in stadiums. Festival staff coordinated these vendors, and many became part of the national tours, standardizing setups and equipment across multiple markets. The stage was the core component, and a custom platform was needed to meet the needs of the ever-touring festivals. Santangelo hired Cincinnati-based Wurzelbacher Construction to develop and build a stage that would enable two acts to be set simultaneously. While one performed, the other could be reset, virtually eliminating downtime between acts. Mark Wurzelbacher (above) and his brothers traveled from city to city, setting and striking the stage, and to this day continue to provide festival staging in Cincinnati (in addition to their many other national special events clients).

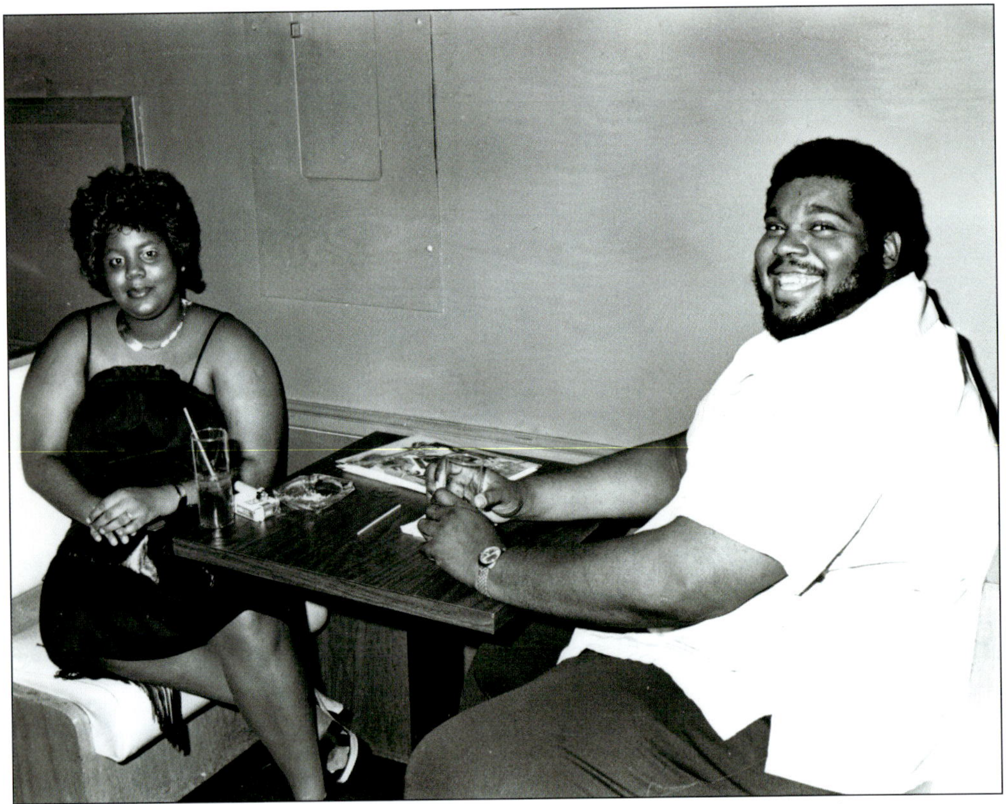

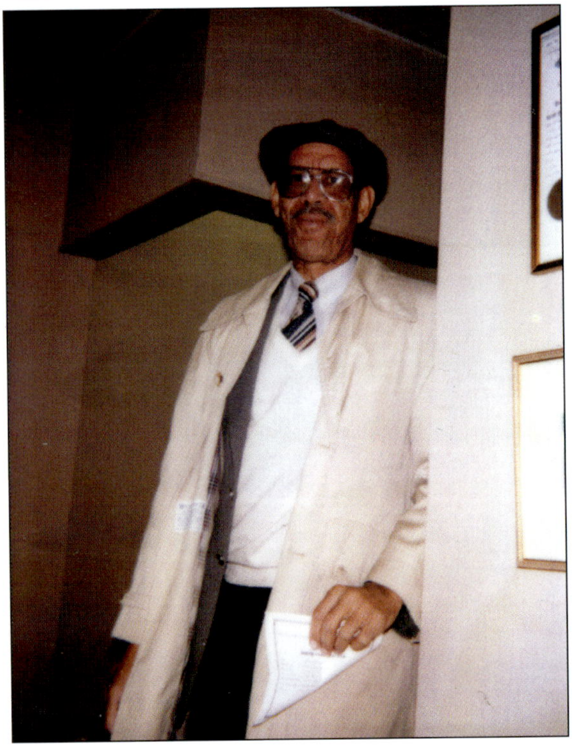

The majority of festival artists received the balance of their pay on the night of the show, often involving large amounts of cash. Tyrone Maupin, son of Cincinnati jazz and blues singer "Popeye" Maupin (above right), joined the festival staff as a bodyguard working under festival security director Rick Rhodes (left). As warm, friendly, and personable as Tyrone could be to his friends, he was a formidable, intimidating presence when necessary.

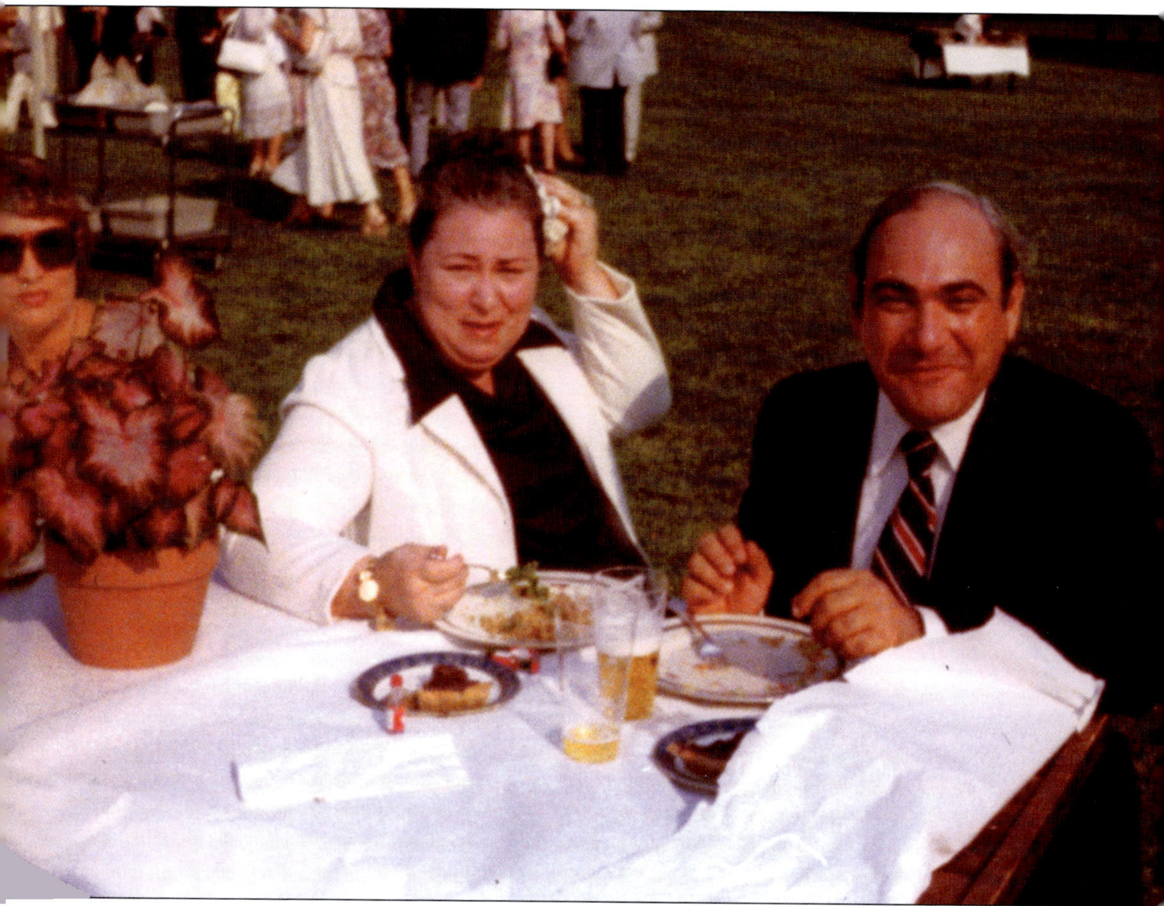

In 1978, at the invitation of Pres. Jimmy Carter, Dino Santangelo (shown above with wife, Jan) joined George Wein on the East Lawn of the White House to celebrate the 50th anniversary of the Newport Jazz Festival. The menu included jambalaya, salad, and pecan pie, but the main course was the entertainment—50 of jazz's greatest performers played for the Carters and their guests.

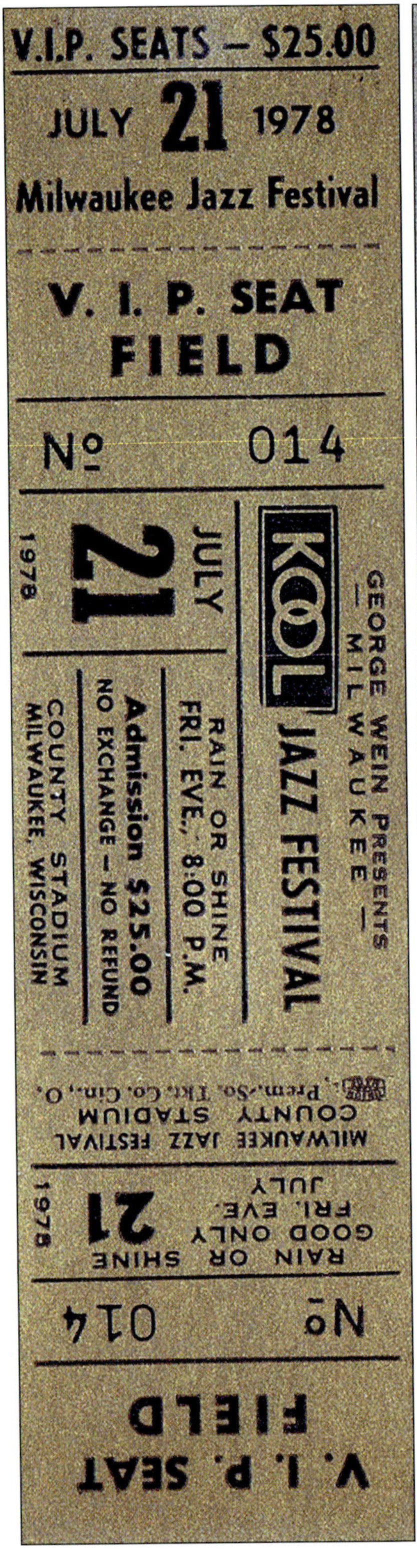

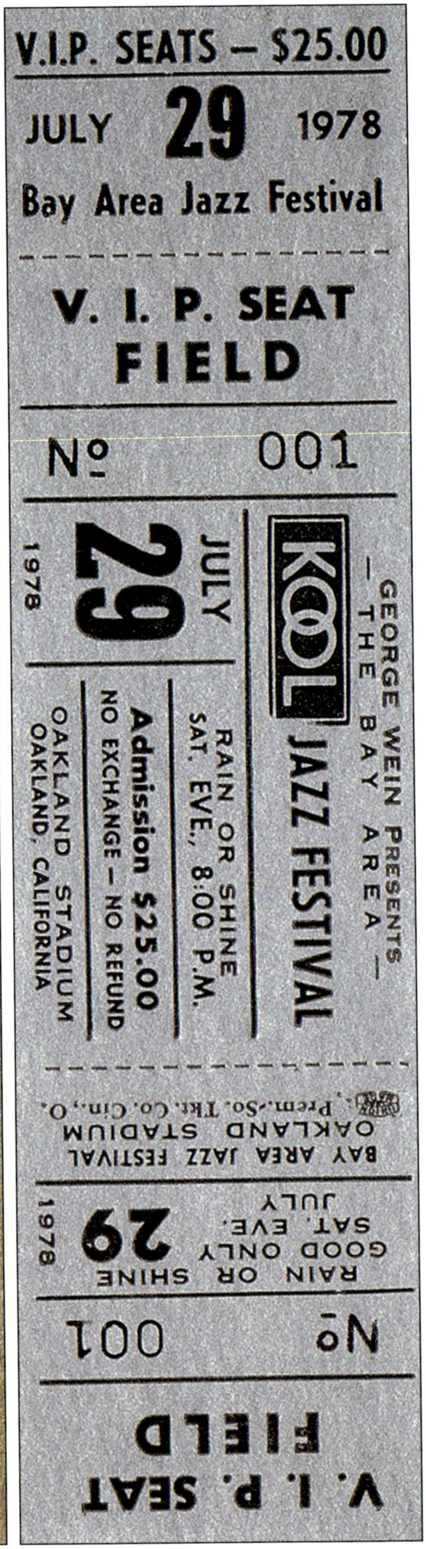

The festival developed unique promotional touches to enhance the experience of its patrons. Field seating was expensive, and VIP seats were even more prestigious, so tickets were designed to reflect the special appeal of these premium sections. The gold and silver tickets were emblematic of that prestige—and in high demand.

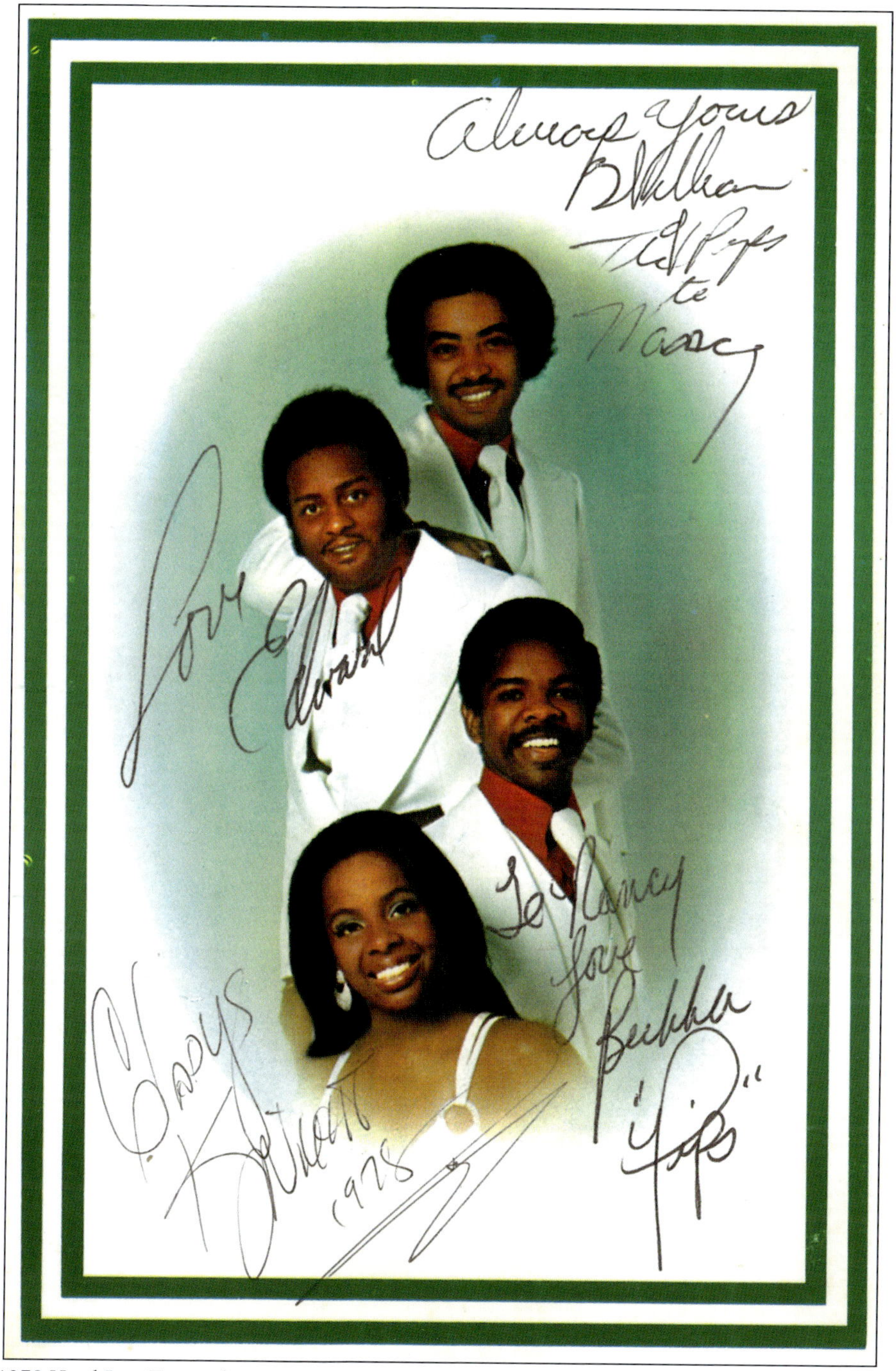

The 1978 Kool Jazz Festival in Cincinnati featured George Benson, the O'Jays, LTD, Al Jarreau, and George Duke on Friday, June 23. Saturday's lineup included Gladys Knight & the Pips (above), Ashford & Simpson, Grover Washington Jr. & Locksmith, Brick, and the Duke Ellington Orchestra (conducted by Mercer Ellington). In Houston, Mayor Jim McConn proclaimed June 9–10, 1978, Kool Jazz Festival Days, "whereas the . . . Festival has been a legend in the entertainment industry and a spectacular event in our city."

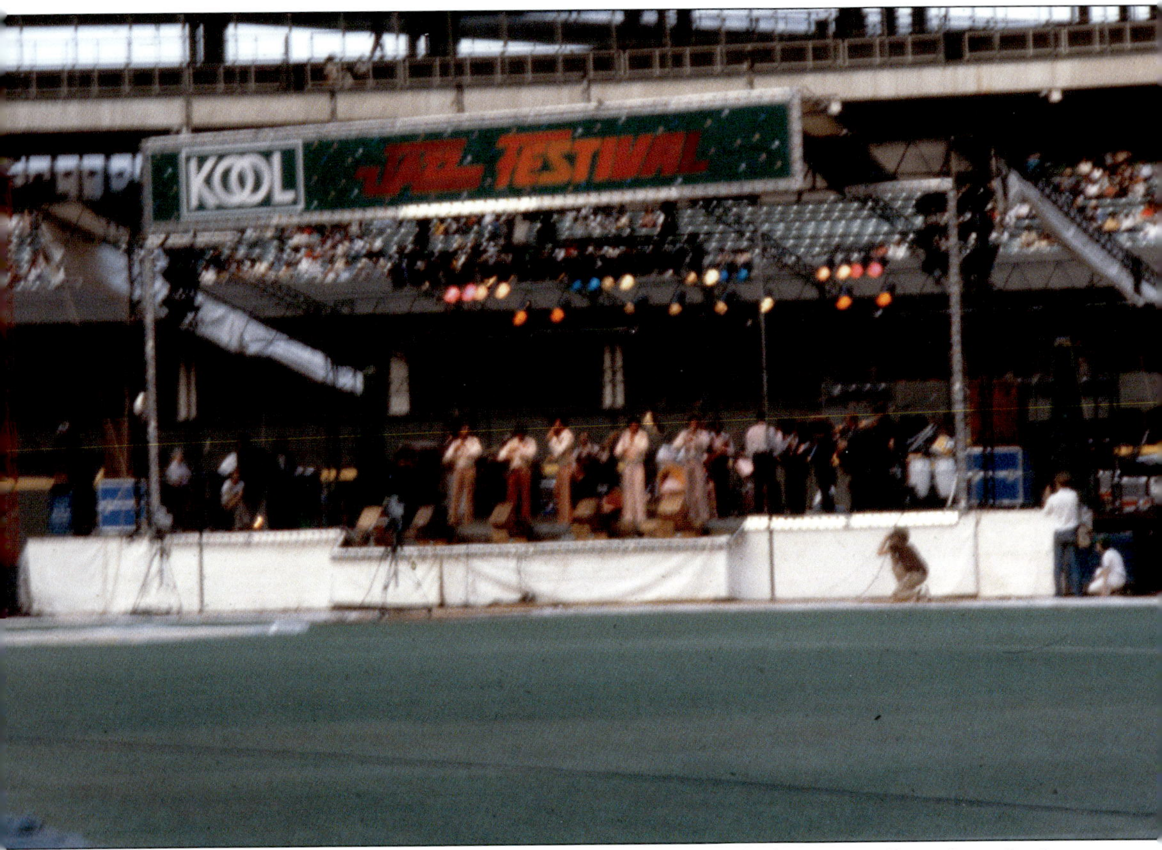

The year 1979 marked the 18th Annual Ohio Valley Jazz Festival. The event at Riverfront Stadium kicked off on Friday, July 20 and featured George Benson, Denise Williams, Rose Royce, Peabo Bryson, and Enchantment. The Saturday show included Ashford & Simpson, the Emotions, Chic, Rick James, and Tavares.

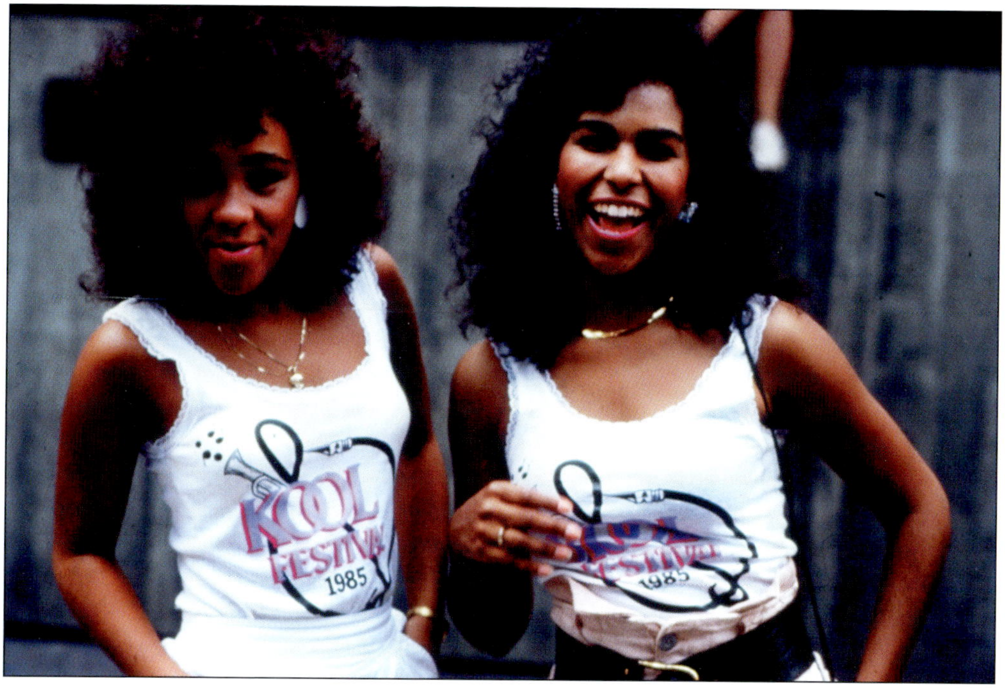

Promoting the festivals was a key to their success, and Santangelo's traditional public relations strategies, combined with the commercial strength of Kool's advertising budget, yielded impressive results. At their peak, the touring Kool Festivals eclipsed the identities of the events in Cincinnati and even Newport as audiences embraced the excitement that swirled around the arrival of the annual programs.

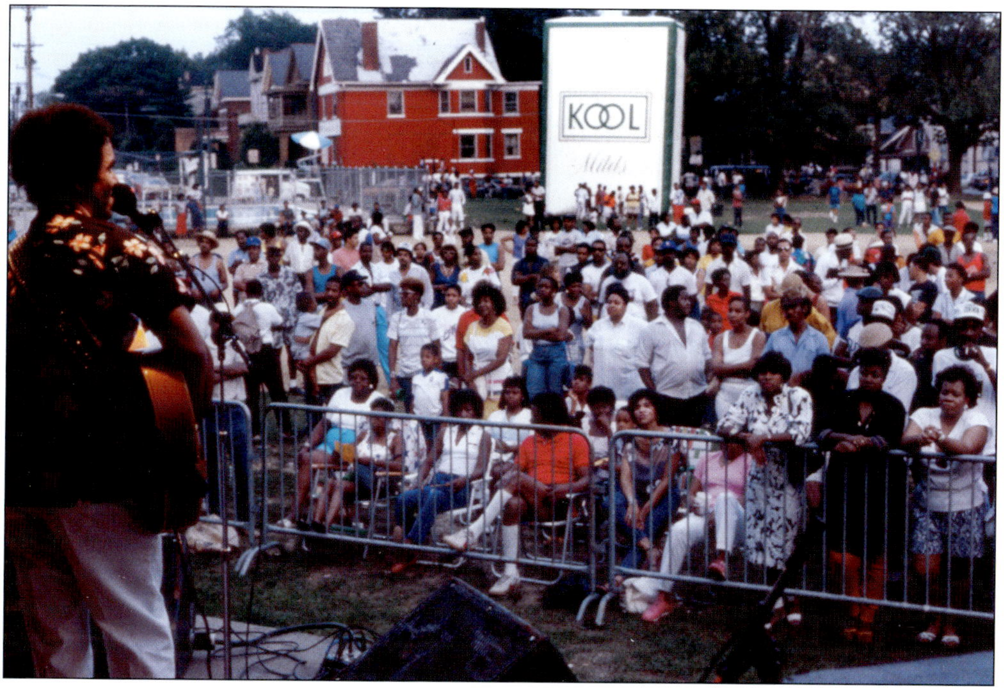

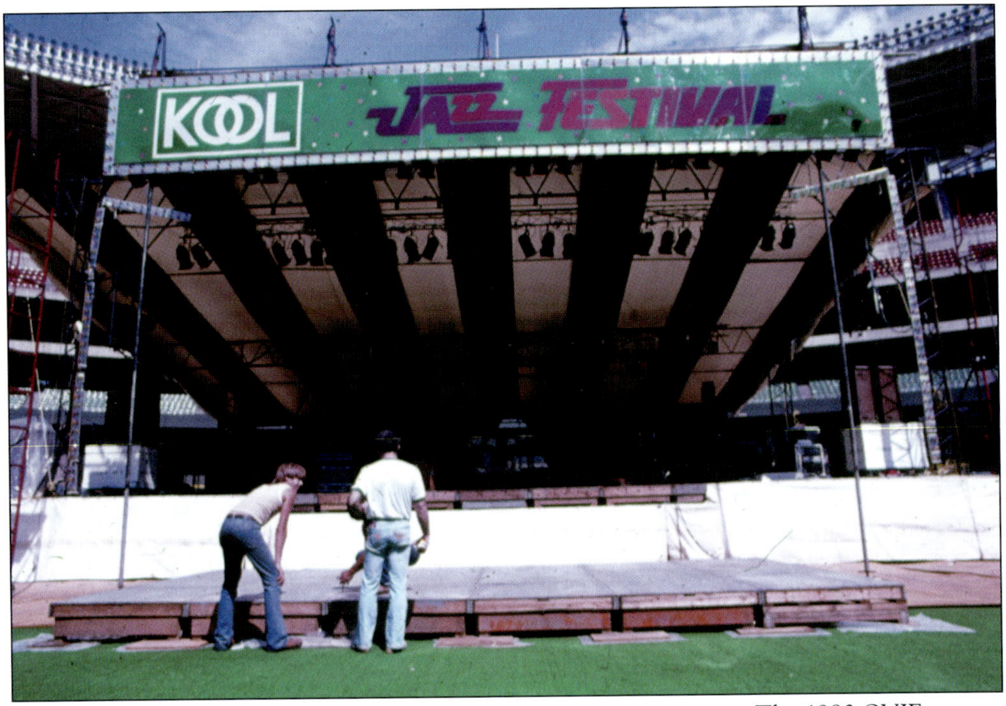

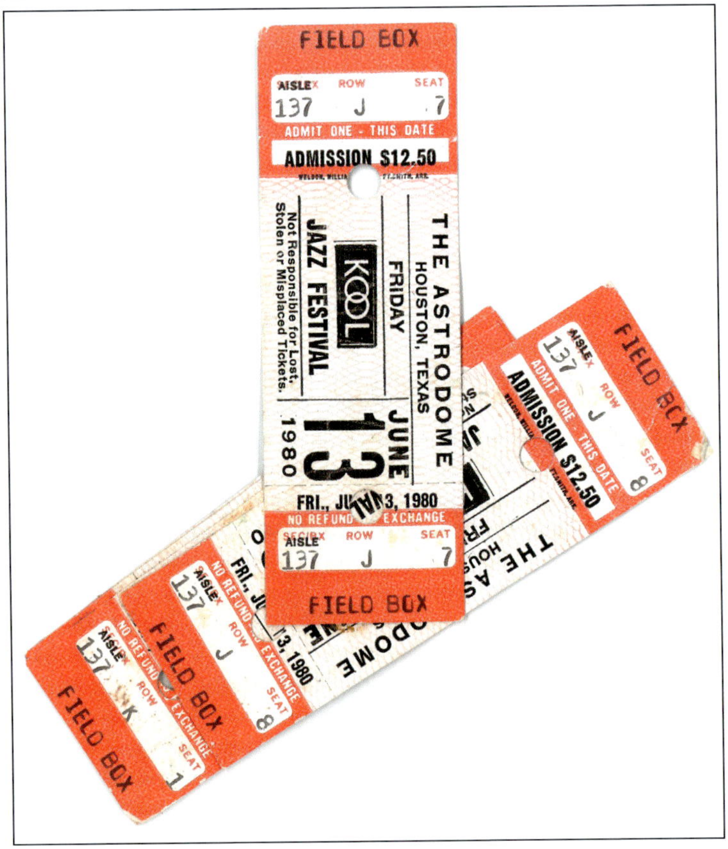

The 1980 OVJF was the 19th in Cincinnati. Artists at Riverfront Stadium on Friday, August 1 included Rufus & Chaka Khan, the Brothers Johnson, Peaches & Herb, B.B. King, Bobby "Blue" Bland, and Cameo. Saturday's show featured Barry White, Chic, Kool & the Gang, Angela Bofill, and the Gap Band. Ticket prices had increased to $12.50, $11.50, and $9. Festival setups were now uniform across the national tour, and stage signage (above) and ticket copy (left) reflected the integration of sponsor branding at every level.

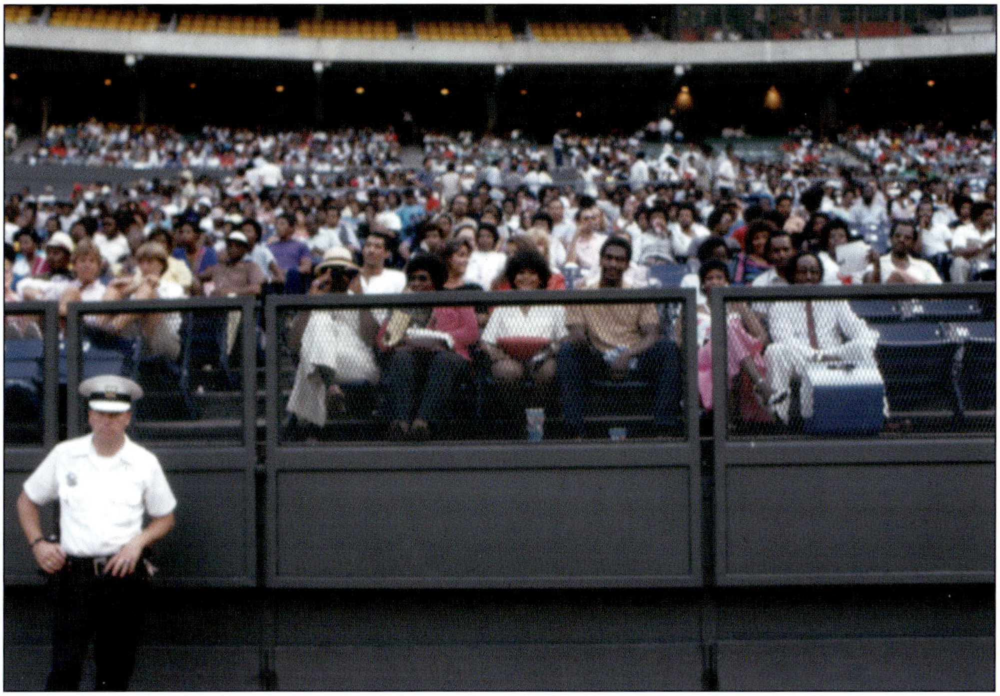

By the 1980s, the Cincinnati Police Department had become one of the biggest fans of the festival. They cited the event as one of the city's least problematic and enjoyed being on the field as much as the patrons who had purchased tickets. As the festival continued to grow in popularity, new problems would arise outside of the stadium as the party continued throughout the city, and heavy traffic would effectively close downtown streets.

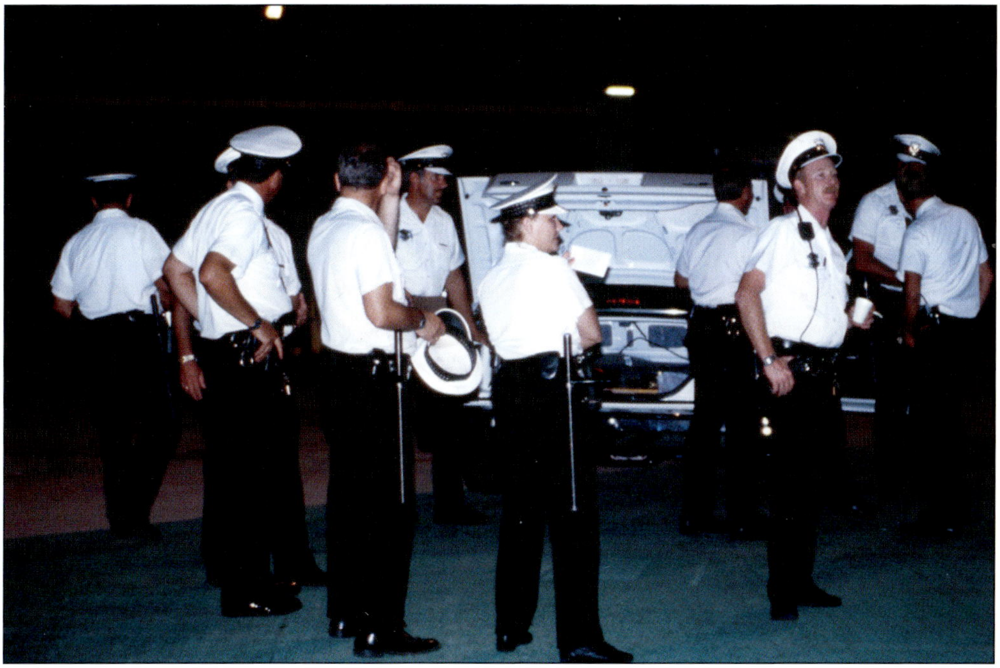

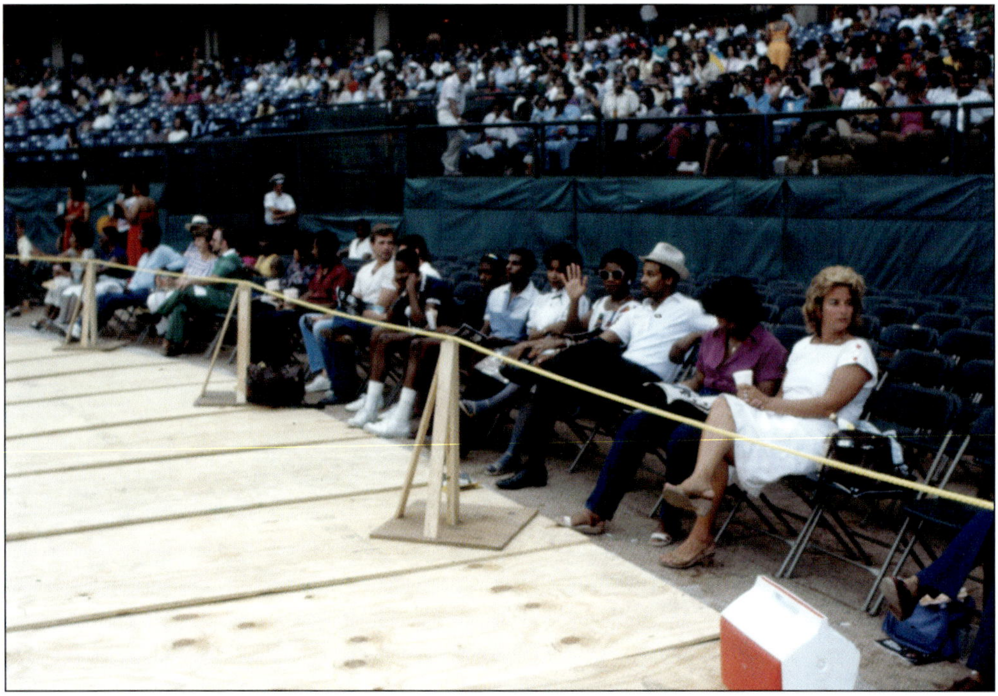

Sitting on the field has always been a preferred option for festival patrons. Special arrangements with stadium management required various forms of ground cover to protect the valuable turf and involved significant expense in addition to the rental of chairs. Informal sections were also added (as shown in these photographs) to accommodate a multitude of other VIP guests.

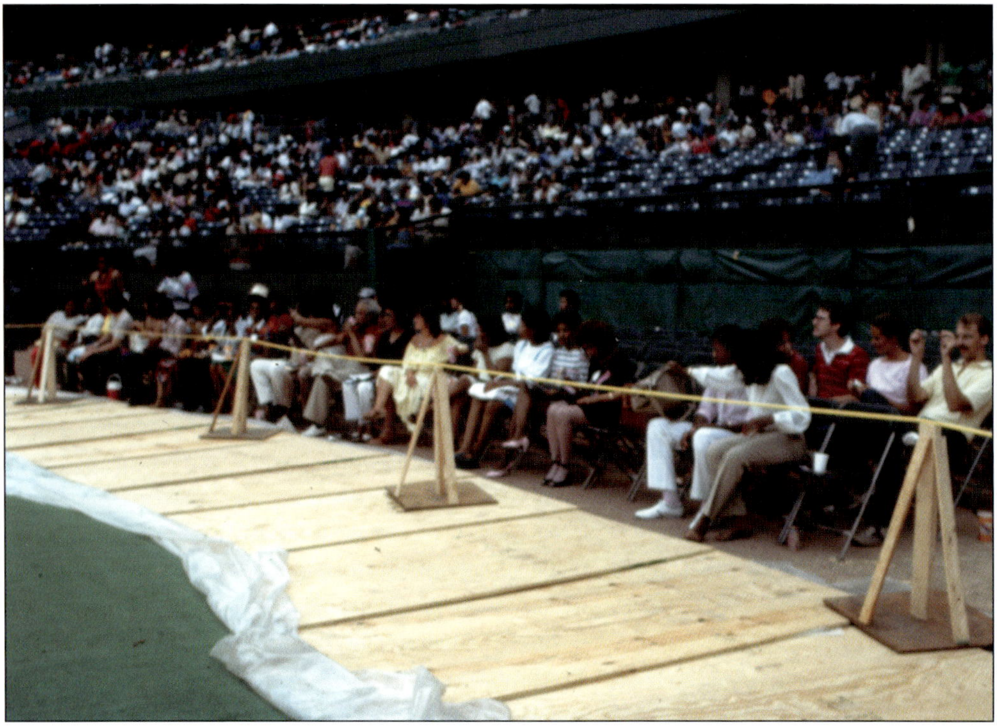

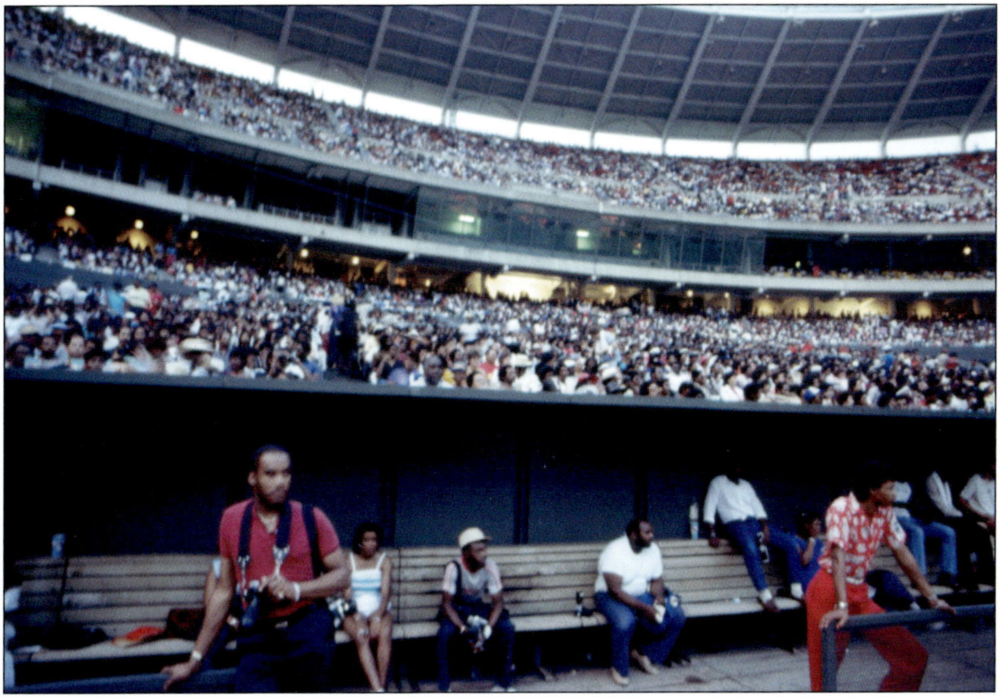

Riverfront Stadium was a "convertible" venue, used for both baseball and football. The festival was held within the baseball season, and the dugouts were made available for the festival staff to use for VIPs and representatives of the media. They also offered convenient connections to backstage areas and dressing rooms and were prestigious places to be seen.

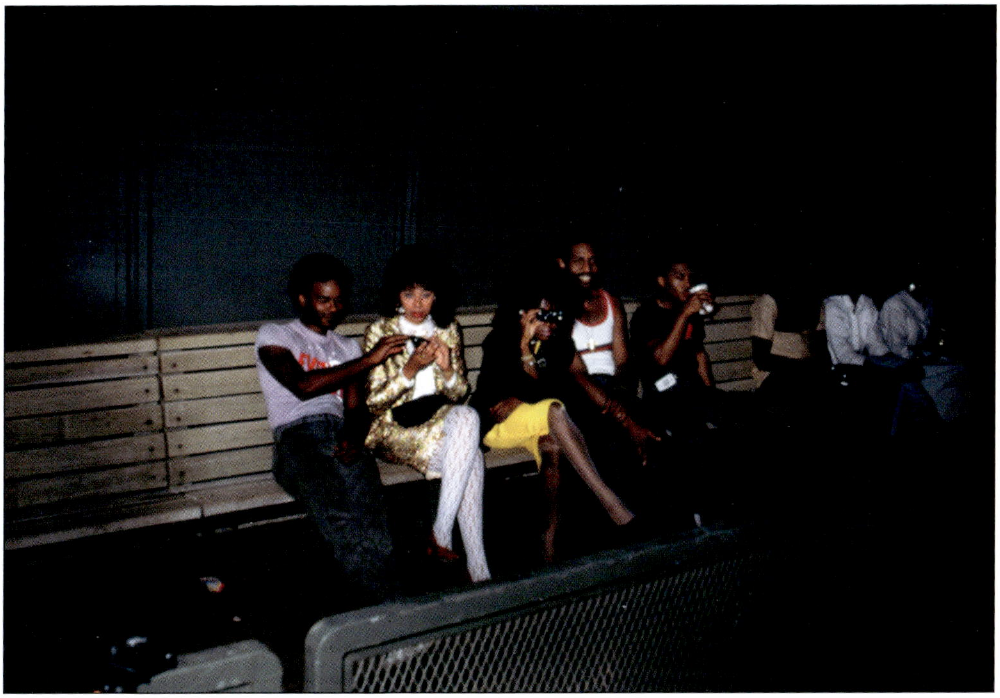

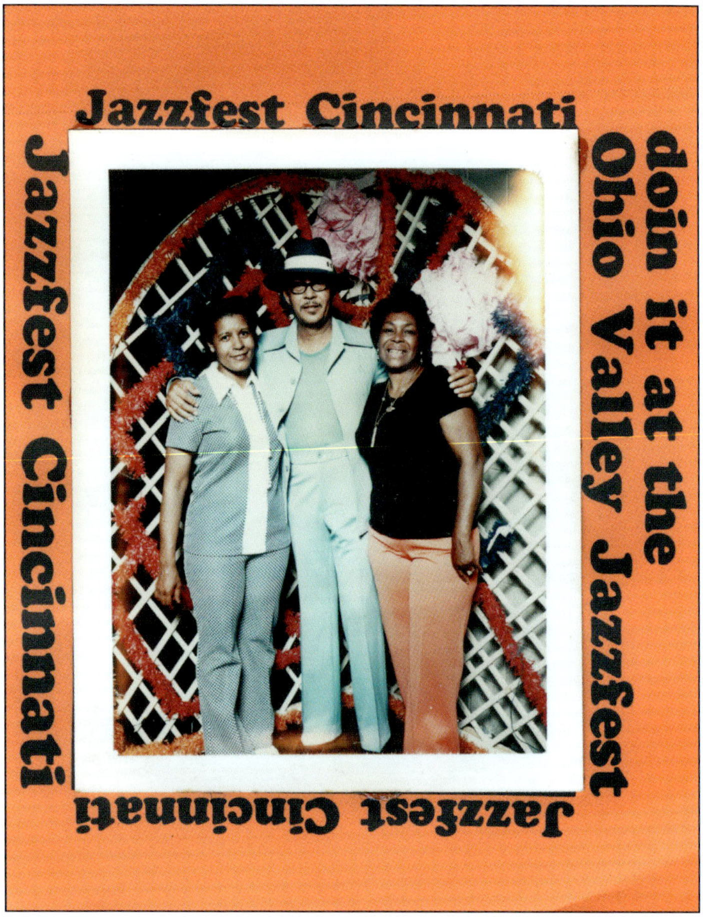

Festival audiences were style conscious, and their clothing reflected the tastes of the times. Souvenir snapshots at the event were very popular. These samples from 1975 display the pride of festival patrons out for a night of fun, great music, and memories.

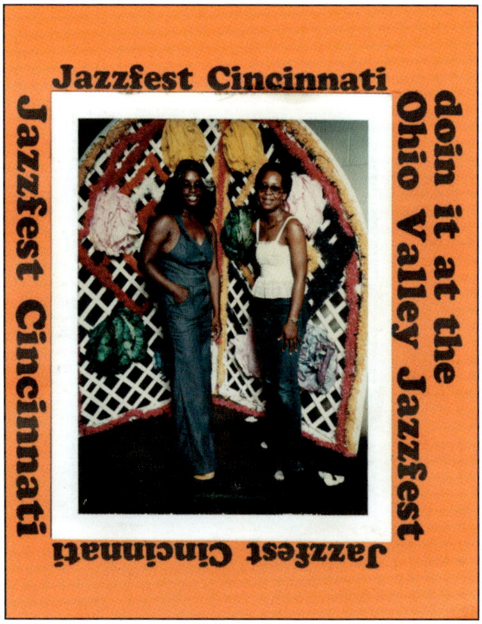

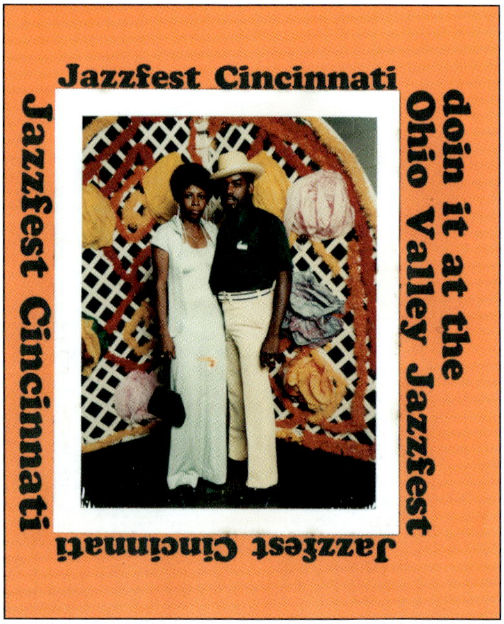

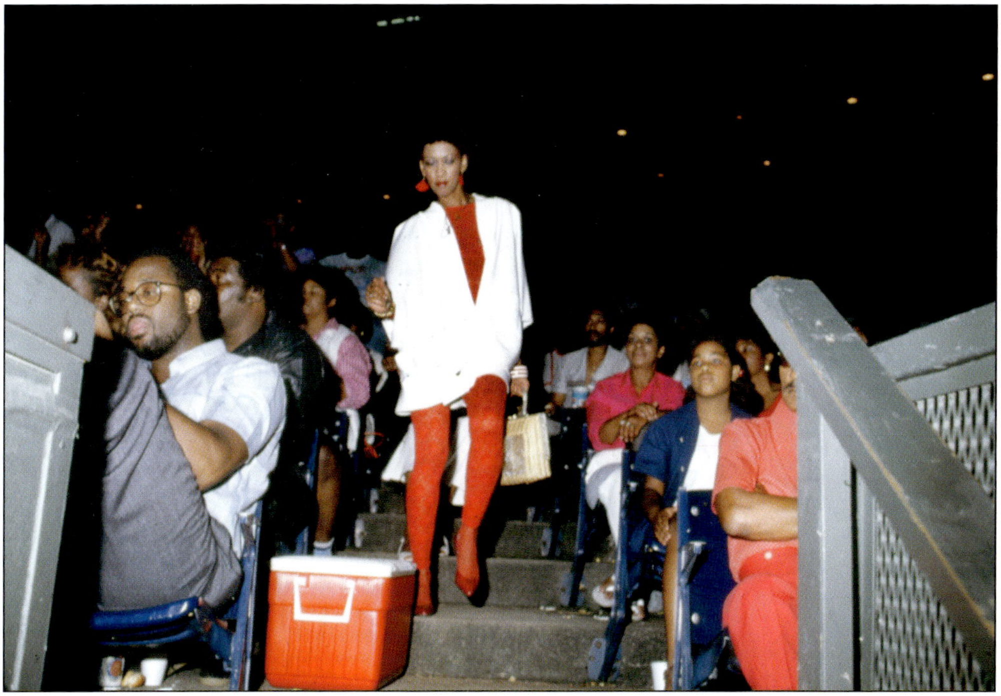

Fashion statements are inherently a reflection of an individual's personal style. Festival weekend in Cincinnati was the time to "step up your game" and be a part of the show—often a colorful part. And while the ladies commanded the most attention, the gentlemen were also well represented.

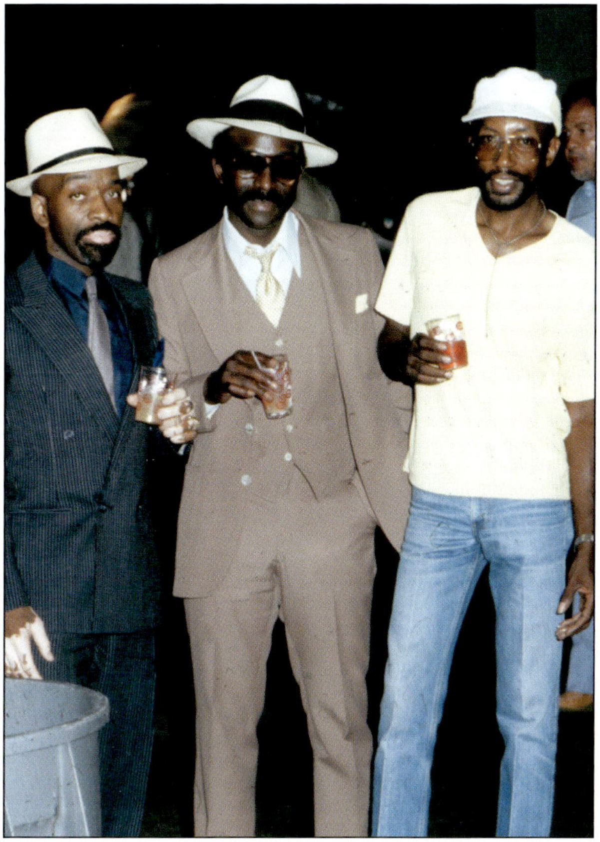

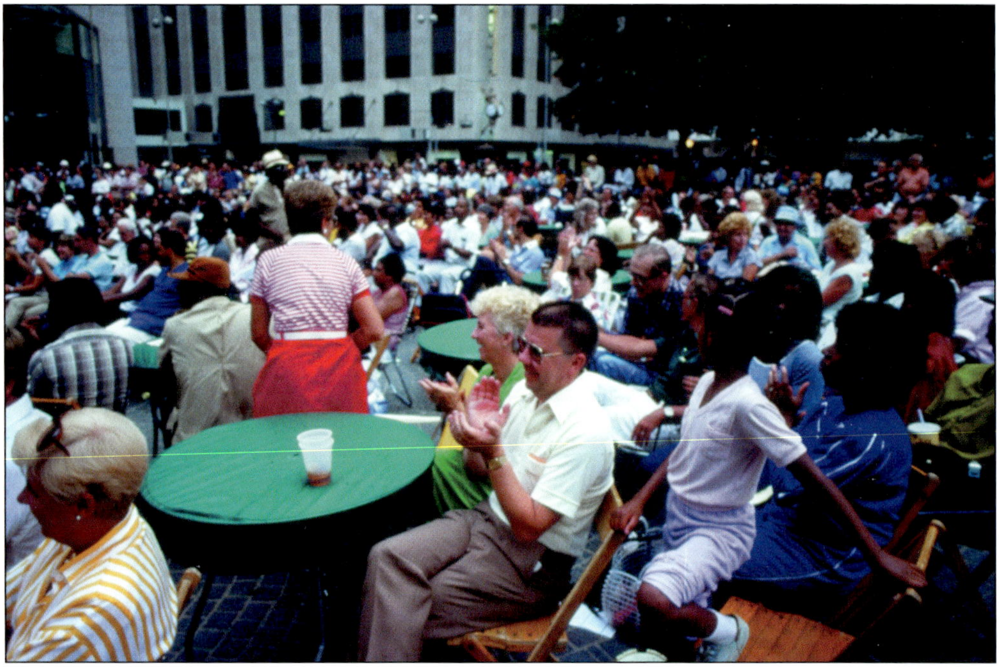

Fashion had always been a big part of the festival experience, but it grew larger as the audience diversified and the event weekend became a real "happening" in Cincinnati. The photograph above shows a fashion show held at Cincinnati's Fountain Square. The colorful outfits of festival patrons were often the subject of news reports and articles and brightened the otherwise drab architecture of Riverfront Stadium (below).

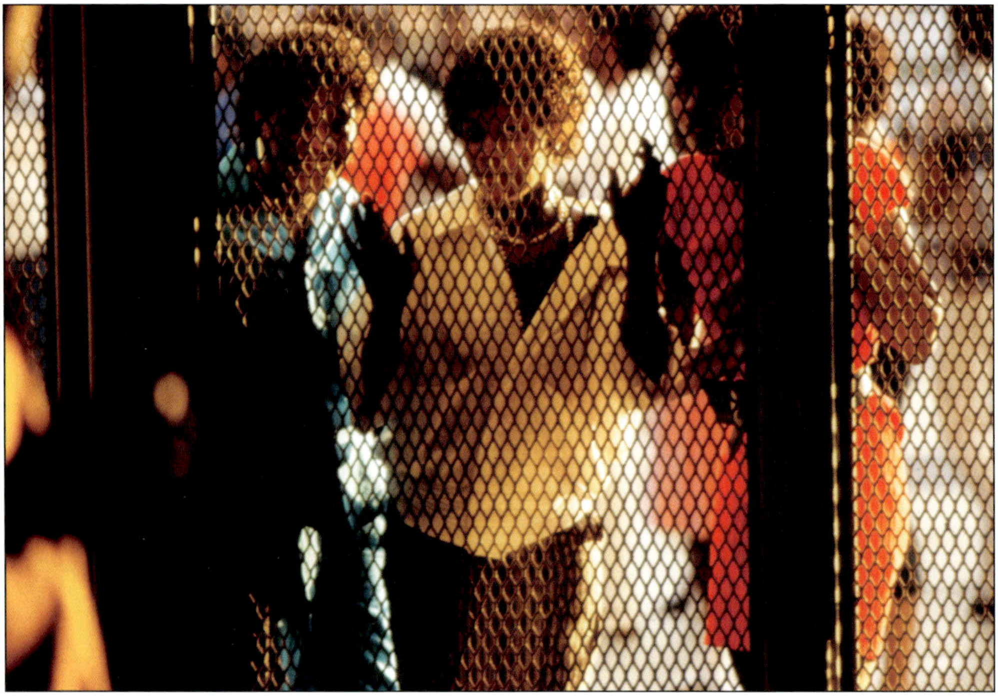

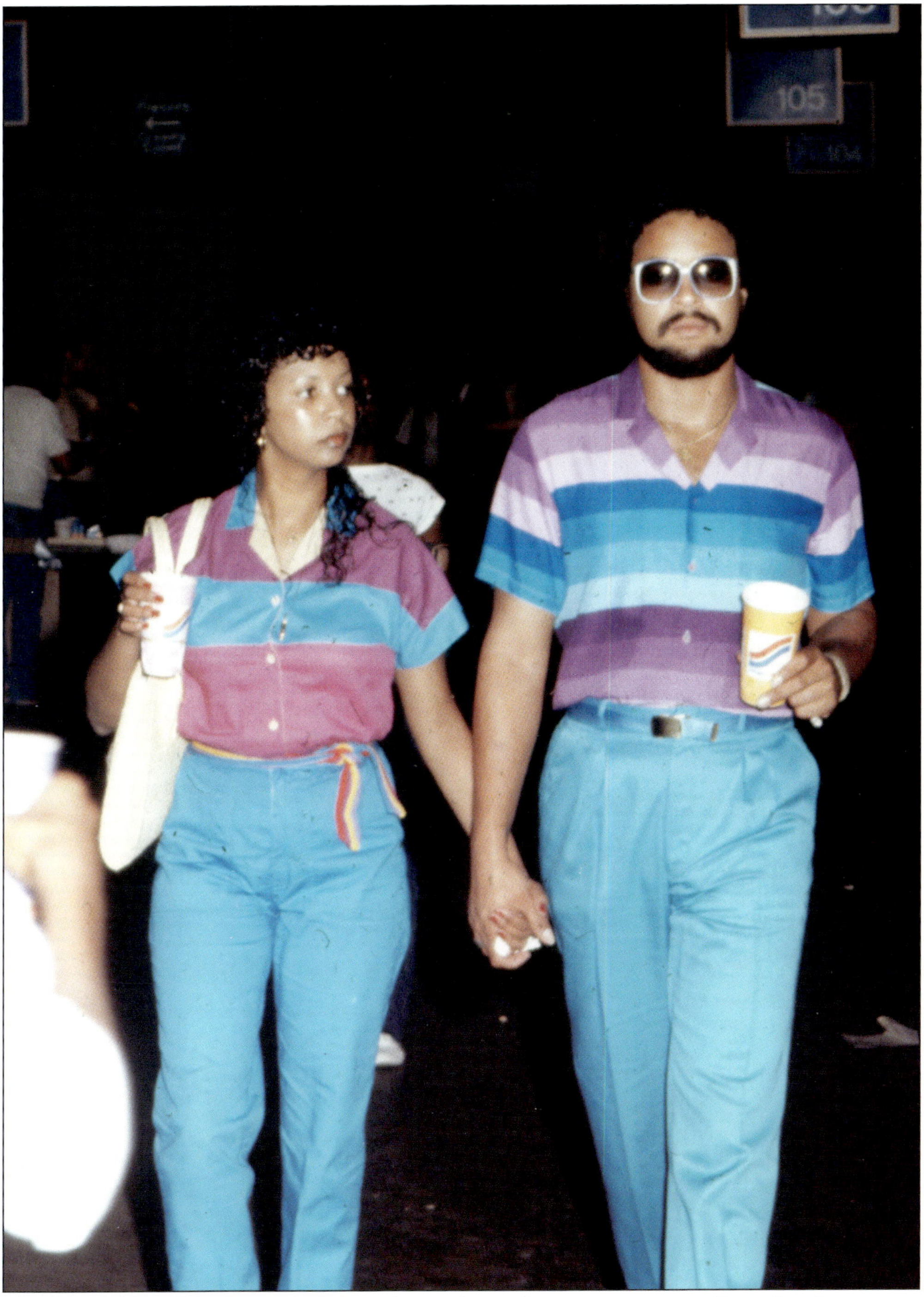

Coordinated couples were a common sight on the stadium concourses on festival nights.

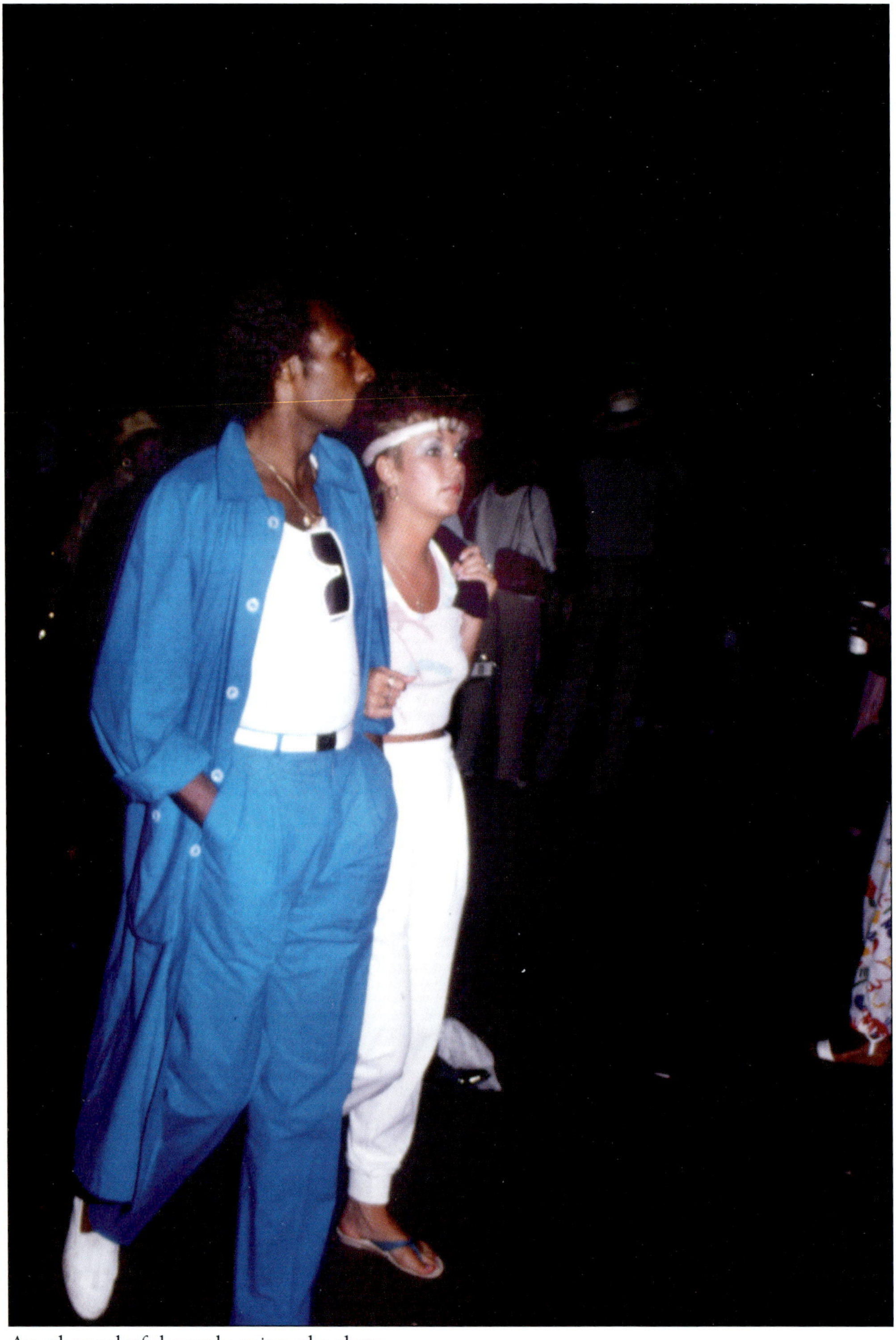

Another colorful couple enjoys the show.

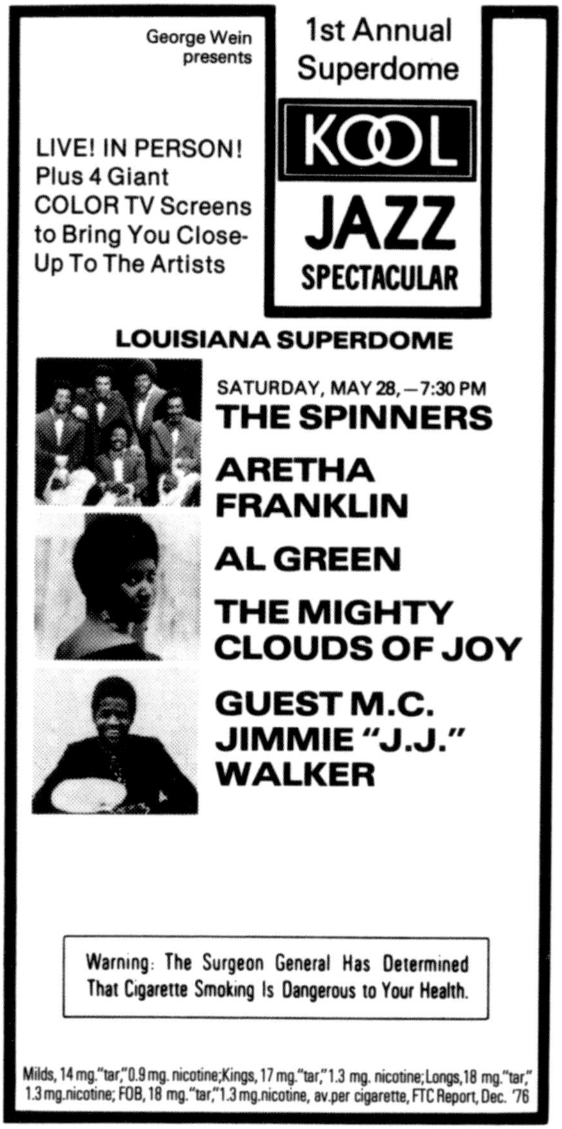

The Kool Festival tours hit major markets across the country, from coast to coast and all points in between. This advertising proof recalls the first concert held at the Superdome, produced by Dino Santangelo's company on behalf of George Wein's Festival Productions, Inc. The event in New Orleans would evolve into the world-famous Jazz & Heritage Festival, which remains an annual fixture on the city's event calendar.

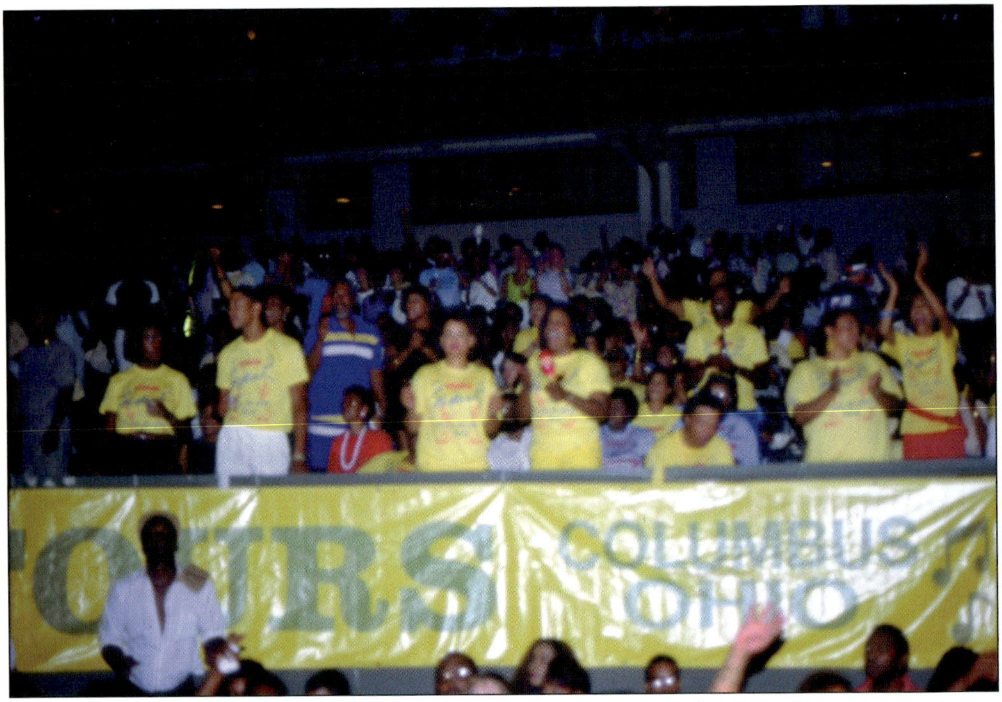

Travel to the festivals became a big business for many entrepreneurs, who created custom experiences that included transportation, premium seats, hotel accommodations, and many other incentives. Tour group organizers were important festival customers, whose seating preferences were taken into account by box office staff. The photographs on this page show M.J. Tours from Columbus, Ohio, whose annual pilgrimage to Cincinnati was complete with banners announcing their presence.

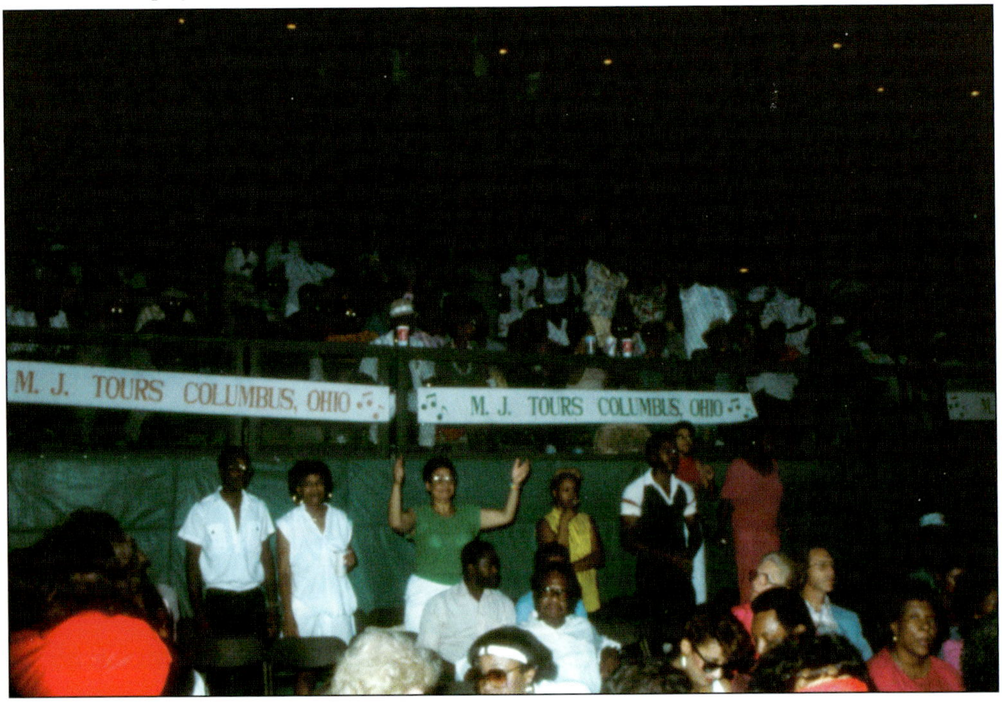

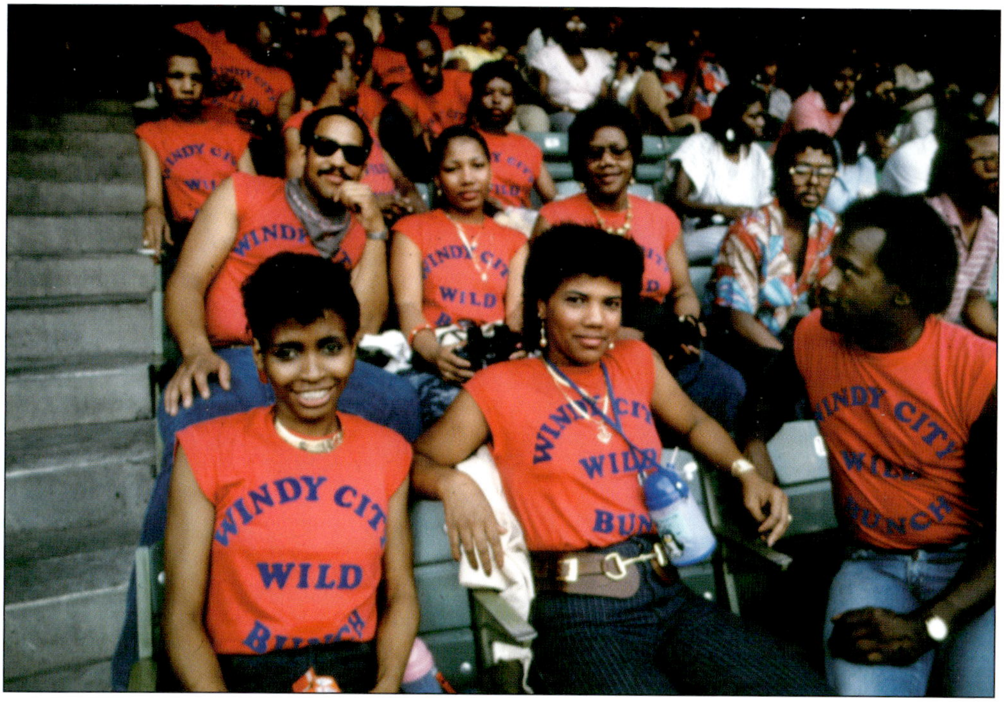

Group organizers, many whose businesses started with their own love of attending the event, developed unique identities complete with T-shirts, banners, pennants, and all sorts of special items to promote themselves and the cities they traveled from.

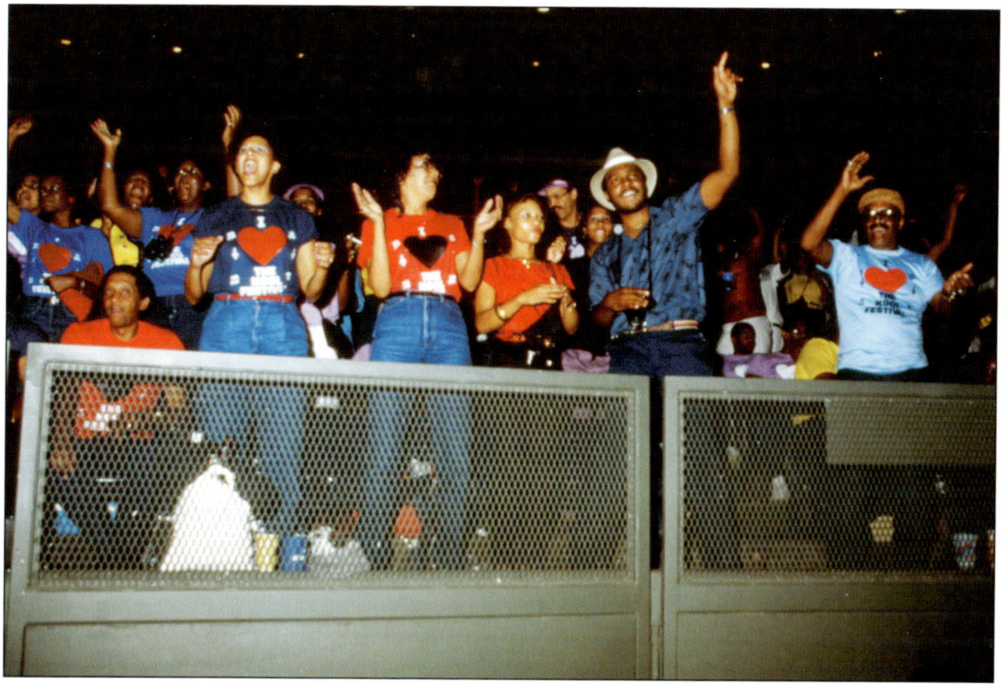

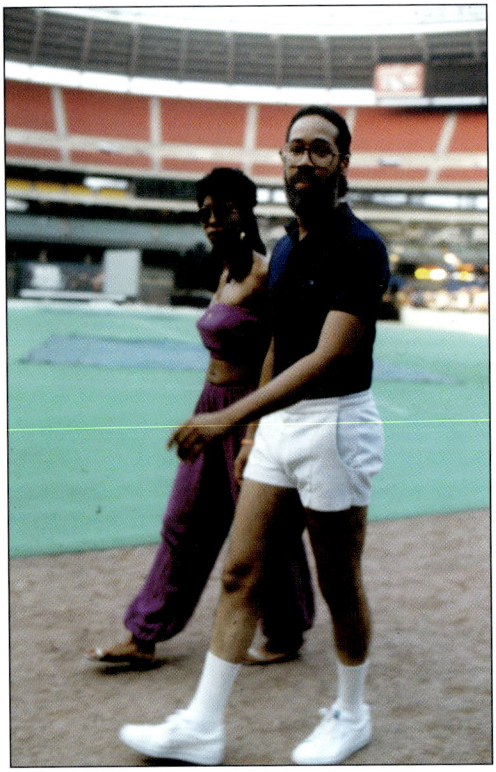

Multiple headliners was the signature of the festival, and artists understood the enormous exposure they would receive through their appearances on festival tours. In the photograph at left, Ashford (Nick) & Simpson (Valerie) check out the Riverfront Stadium setup before their performance in 1980. The photograph below shows Charlie Wilson, cofounder of the Gap Band.

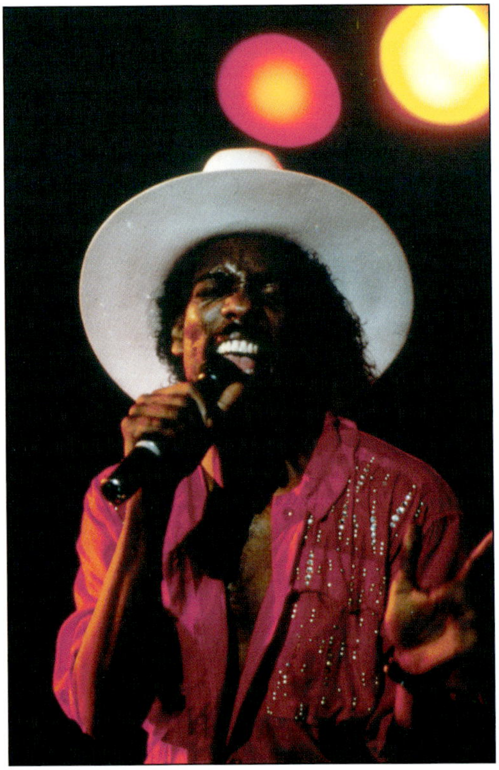

Six

1981–1985

The End of an Era

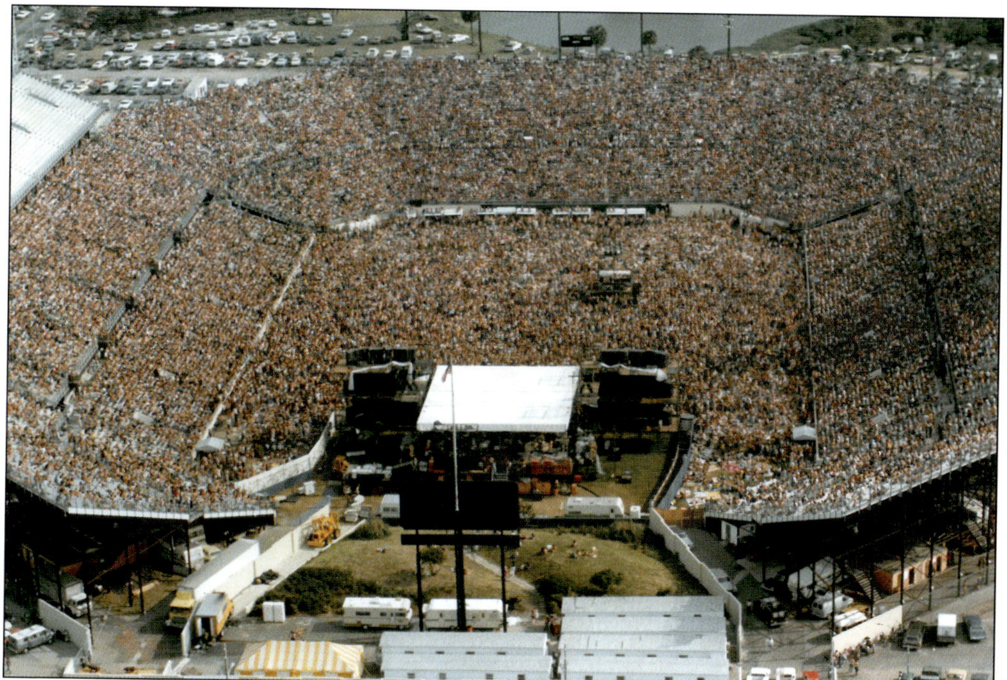

The festival's 20th anniversary was held on July 31 and August 1, 1981. MC Tim Reid, better known as the character he played on *WKRP in Cincinnati*, Venus Flytrap, introduced the artists. Friday featured the O'Jays, Cameo, Peabo Bryson, The Temptations, and the Ohio Jazz All Stars (Herbie Mann, Nat Adderley, Jimmy Smith, and Eddie "Lockjaw" Davis). Saturday's acts included Aretha Franklin, the Spinners, Kool & the Gang, the Manhattans, and Art Blakey & the Jazz Messengers. At the festival in Orlando that year (above), a capacity crowd was the result of a massive ticket counterfeiting scheme that led to a lawsuit against the City of Orlando (which had controlled the printing of tickets, as well as day-of-show procedures and personnel). As the ticket "drop" came in to be counted, Atlanta promoter and Orlando investor J. Lee Friedman quickly realized many were bogus.

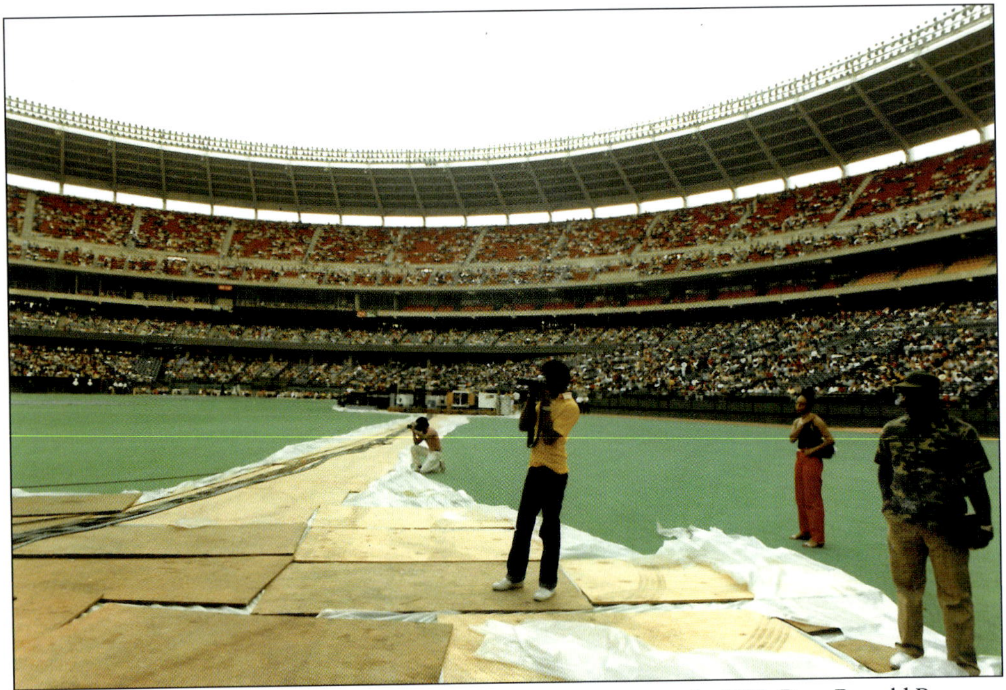

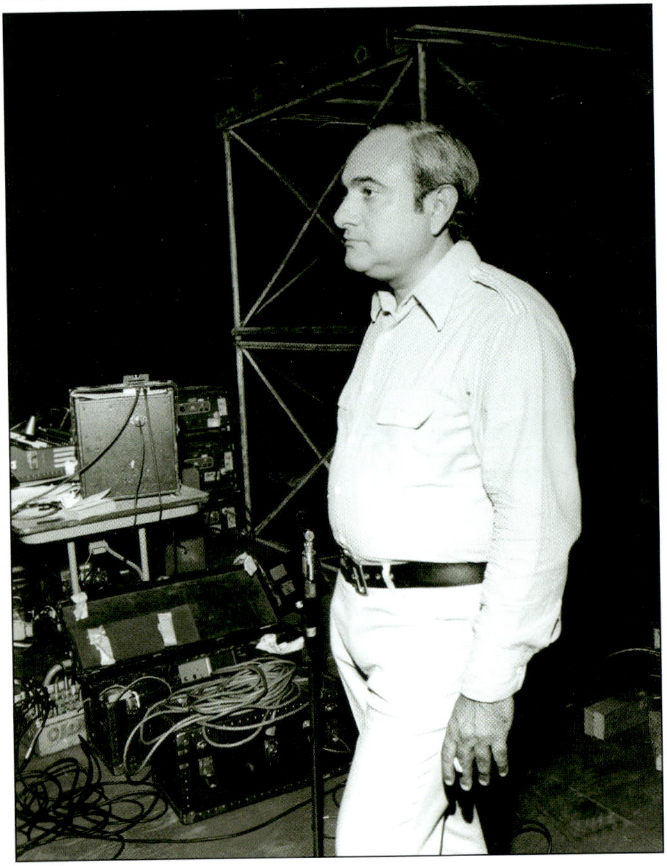

In 1981, Pres. Ronald Reagan sent the Ohio Valley Kool Jazz Festival his congratulations on its 20th anniversary. Ohio governor Jim Rhodes would also recognize Dino Santangelo's role in a formal citation: "It is a pleasure . . . to recognize and honor outstanding individuals whose achievements have significantly benefited our State . . . Dino organized summer outdoor concerts featuring big names in the jazz field . . . and brought recognition to the black community, honoring the contributions they have made to our culture." The acknowledgments were well deserved. Santangelo (left) had successfully navigated the festival through two turbulent decades.

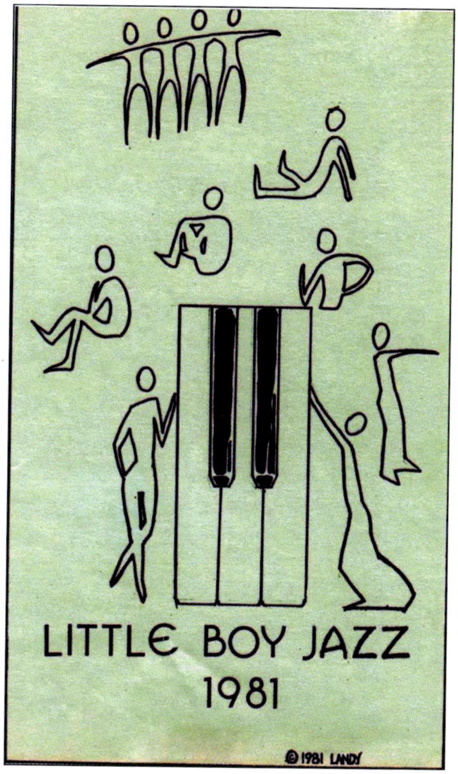

Restaurants and hotels were not the only local enterprises to get a boost from the event. The festival supported local artists, musicians, photographers, and creative types like Arzell Nelson, who received support and encouragement from Dino Santangelo for his idea to produce a play. His self-written and produced musical *Little Boy Jazz* premiered on the stage of the prestigious Cincinnati Playhouse to critical acclaim.

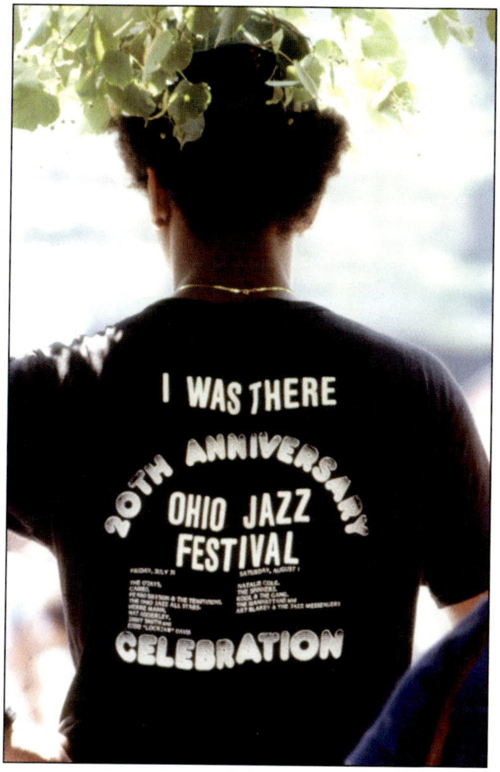

Bootleg T-shirts were always popular, especially for the festival's anniversary concerts. While independent vendor-produced merchandise presented copyright and other challenges, it simply reflected the depth of support the event commanded, and resourceful entrepreneurs were quick to capitalize on the desire for festival souvenirs.

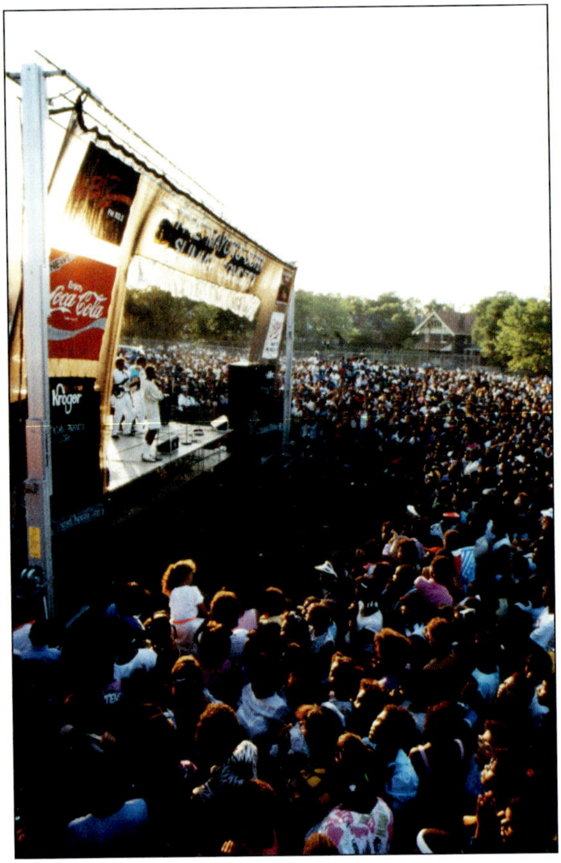

Community events held in connection with the festivals were popular and drew huge crowds. These photographs show one such event in Cincinnati in 1985, sponsored by the Cincinnati Recreation Commission and featuring performing artist Roxanne. Not everyone could afford to attend the concerts at the stadium, but the free concerts enabled thousands of people to join in the celebration that the festival weekend had become.

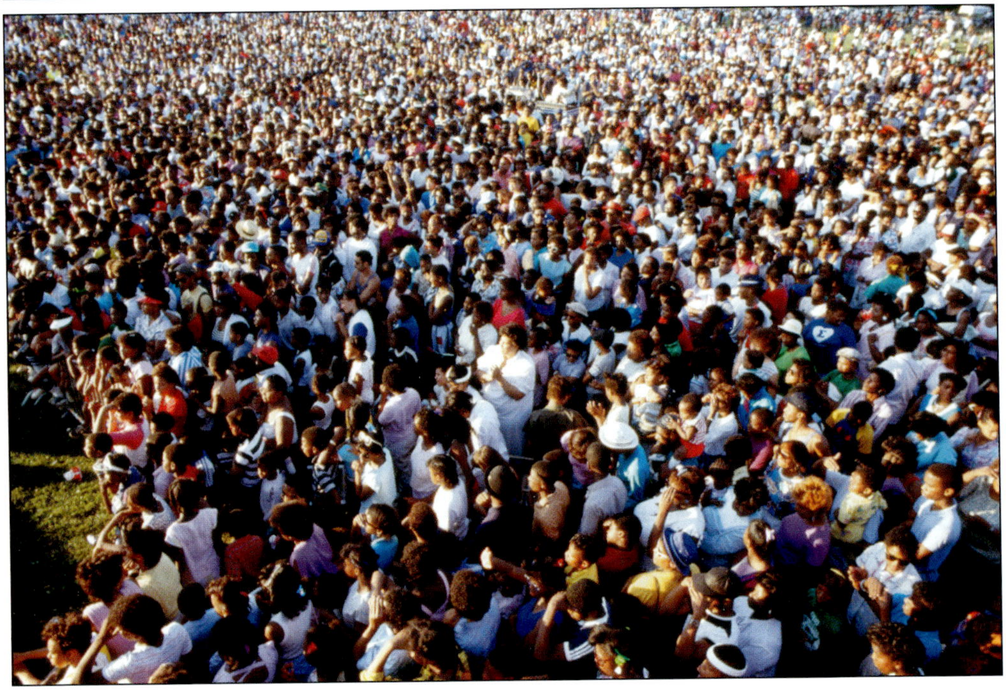

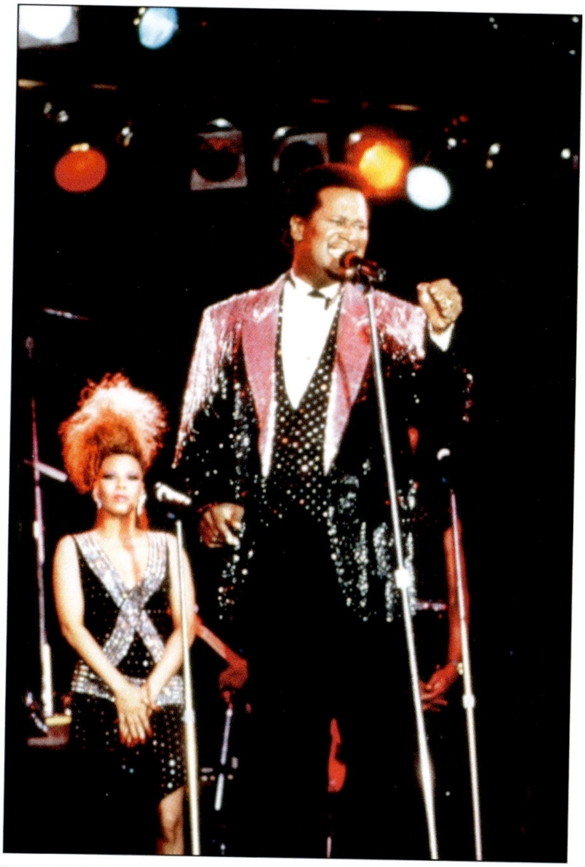

The 21st Cincinnati lineup in 1982 was the first to feature a rising musical star named Luther Vandross (right), who would go on to become the biggest ticket seller in festival history. He was in good company; on Friday, July 16, acts included George Benson, Al Jarreau, Lee Ritenour, Herbie Hancock, and Maynard Ferguson & his Orchestra. Saturday's show featured Vandross, the Commodores, Kool & the Gang, Sister Sledge, Lakeside, and Skyy. Below, Darnell Coleman performed at Cincinnati's Fountain Square as part of the festival's weekend celebration. (Both, courtesy of Michael Mitchell.)

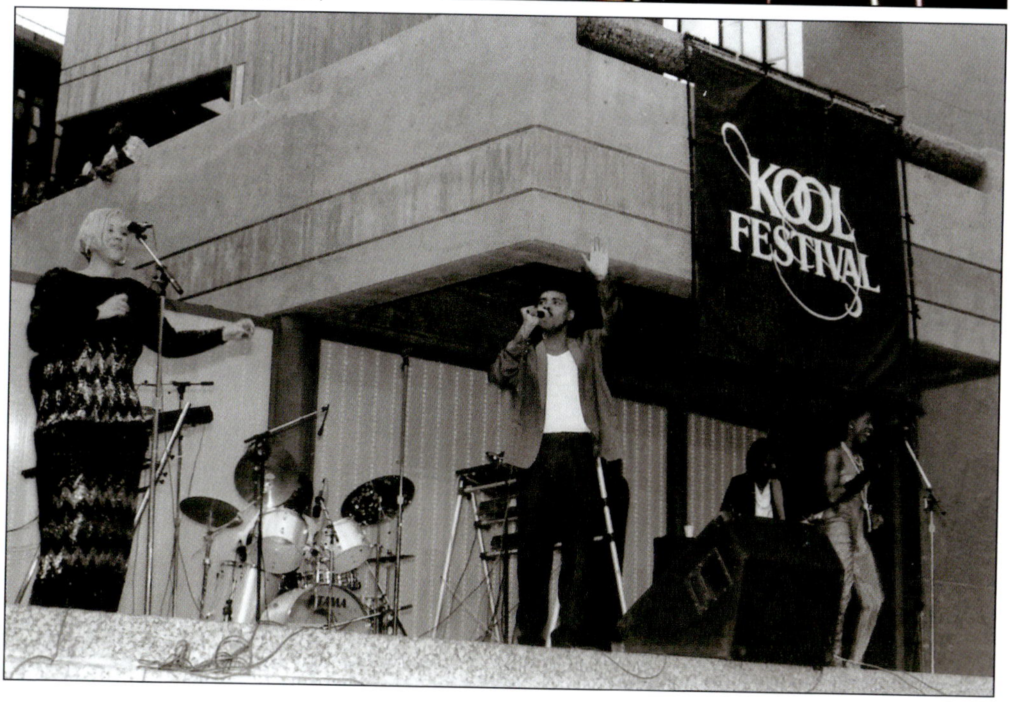

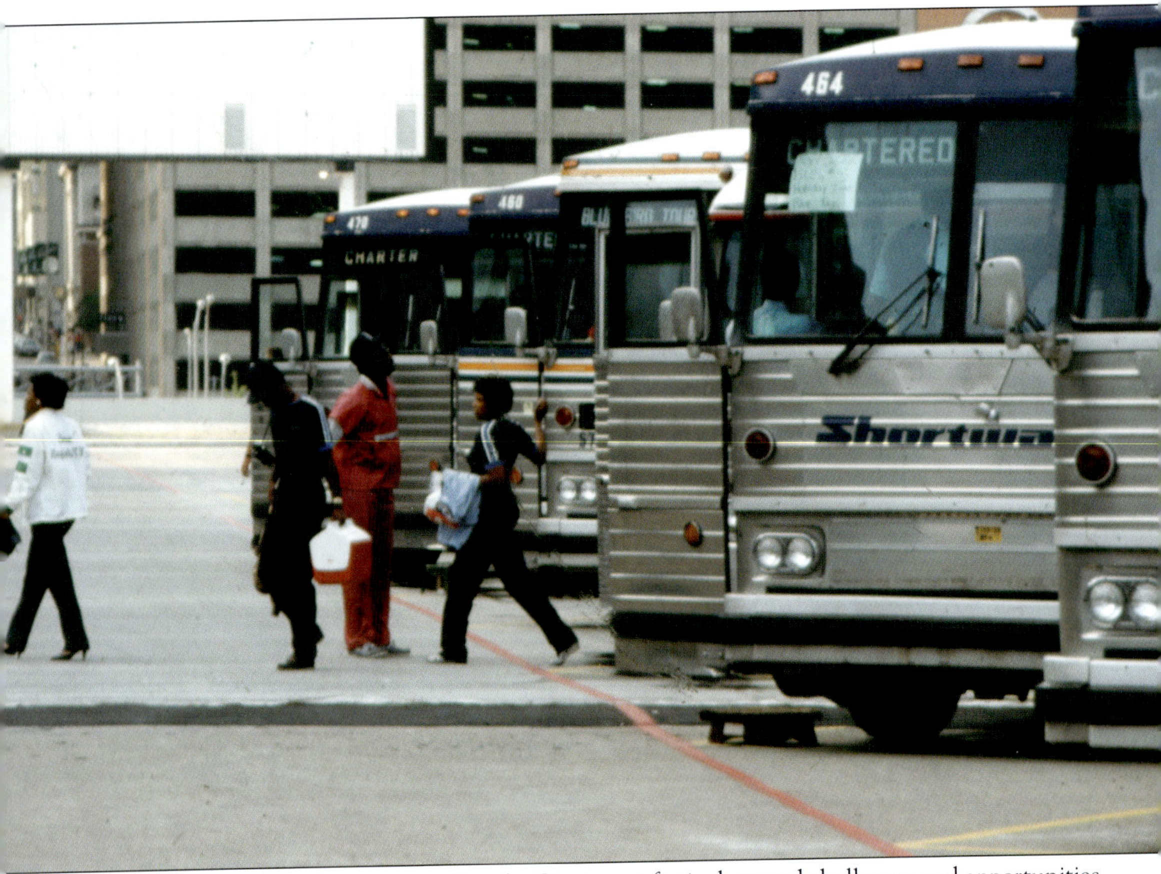

The large number of groups attending the Cincinnati festival created challenges and opportunities. Tour group organizers, bus charter companies, and the festival's staff helped coordinate limited parking on the concourse of Riverfront Stadium, ultimately under the control of stadium management. (Courtesy of Mel Grier.)

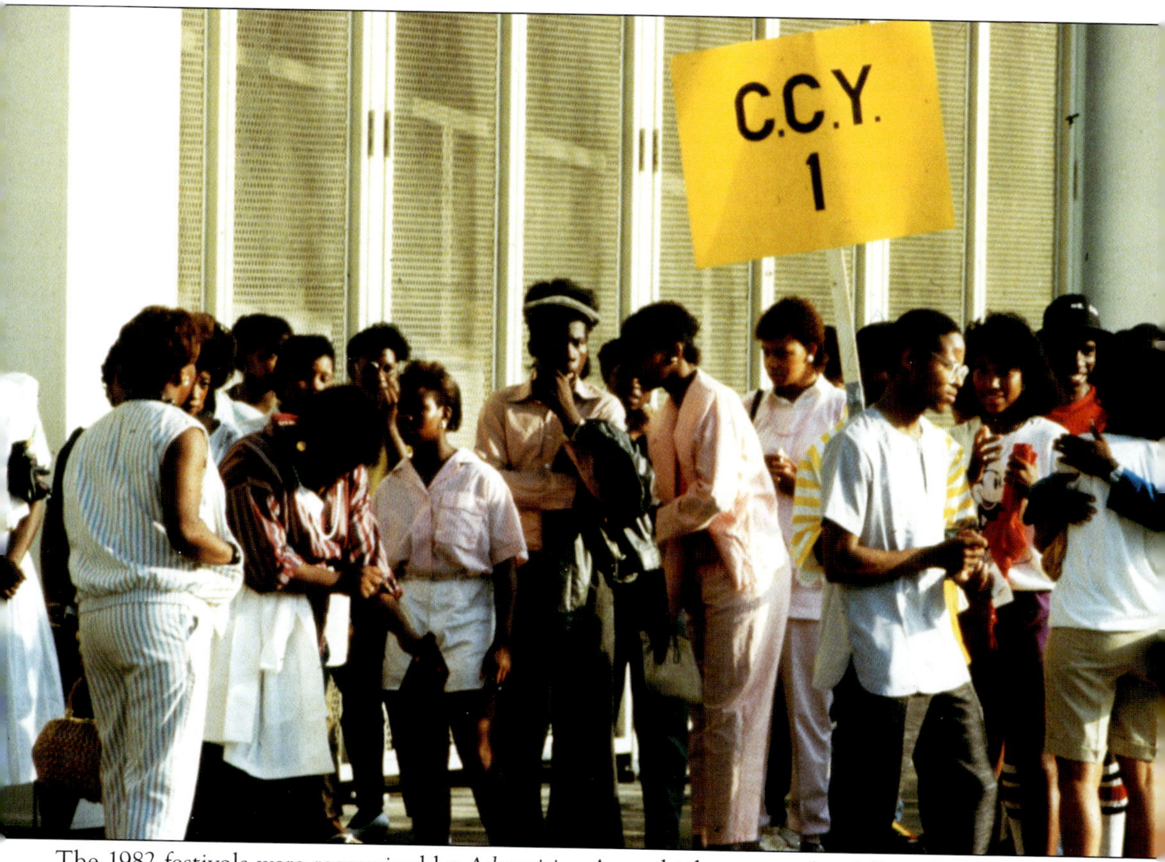

The 1982 festivals were recognized by *Advertising Age*, which congratulated Dino Santangelo on the Kool Jazz Festivals being named one of the Outstanding Promotions of the Year. Shown above is a group with the Citizens' Committee on Youth, an organization developed to help kids connect to summer jobs through a popular "Rent A Kid" program. The Cincinnati festival had a long tradition of ticket donations to worthy causes, and by this means, many young people had the opportunity to see the biggest concert event of the year.

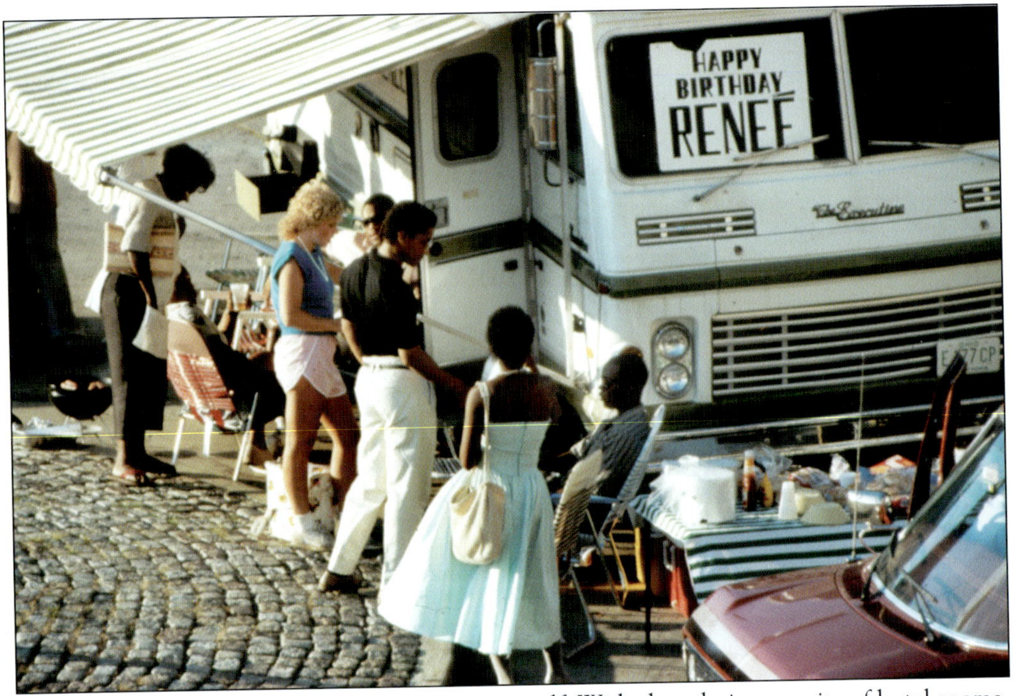

Tailgating at the festival grew to be an event in itself. With the relative scarcity of hotel rooms, creative patrons found the experience of traveling to Cincinnati could put them front and center at the stadium in ways that made up for the inconvenience. Reservations for plaza-level parking were limited, and competition for those opportunities could be fierce. But on the weekend of the event, it was all harmony, fun, and excitement. Local photographer Mel Grier captured these moments in 1982. His images reflect the activities leading up to the event and, often, the shared experience of simply getting there. (Both, courtesy of Mel Grier.)

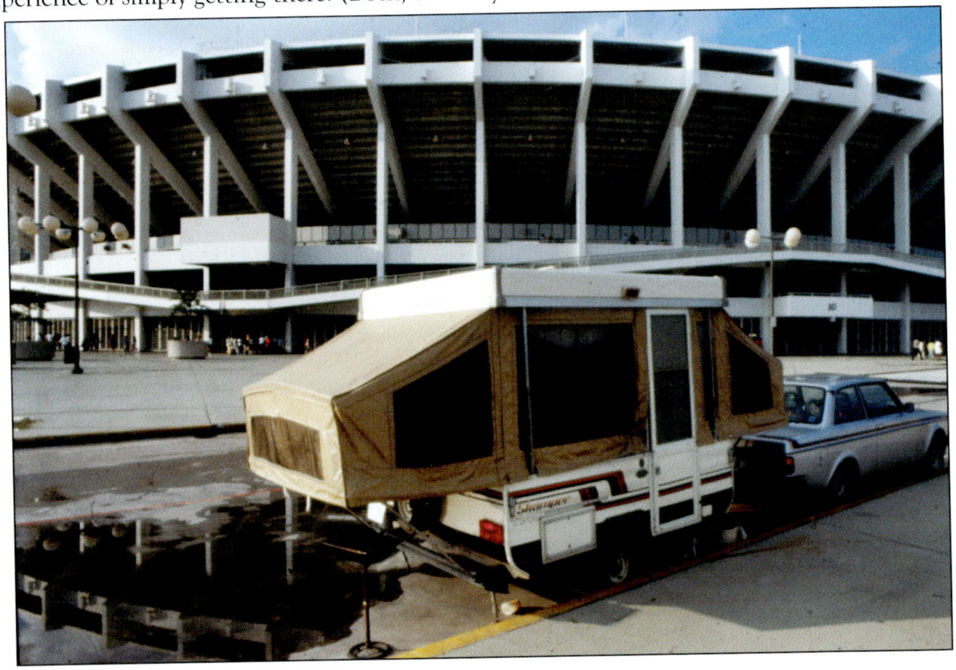

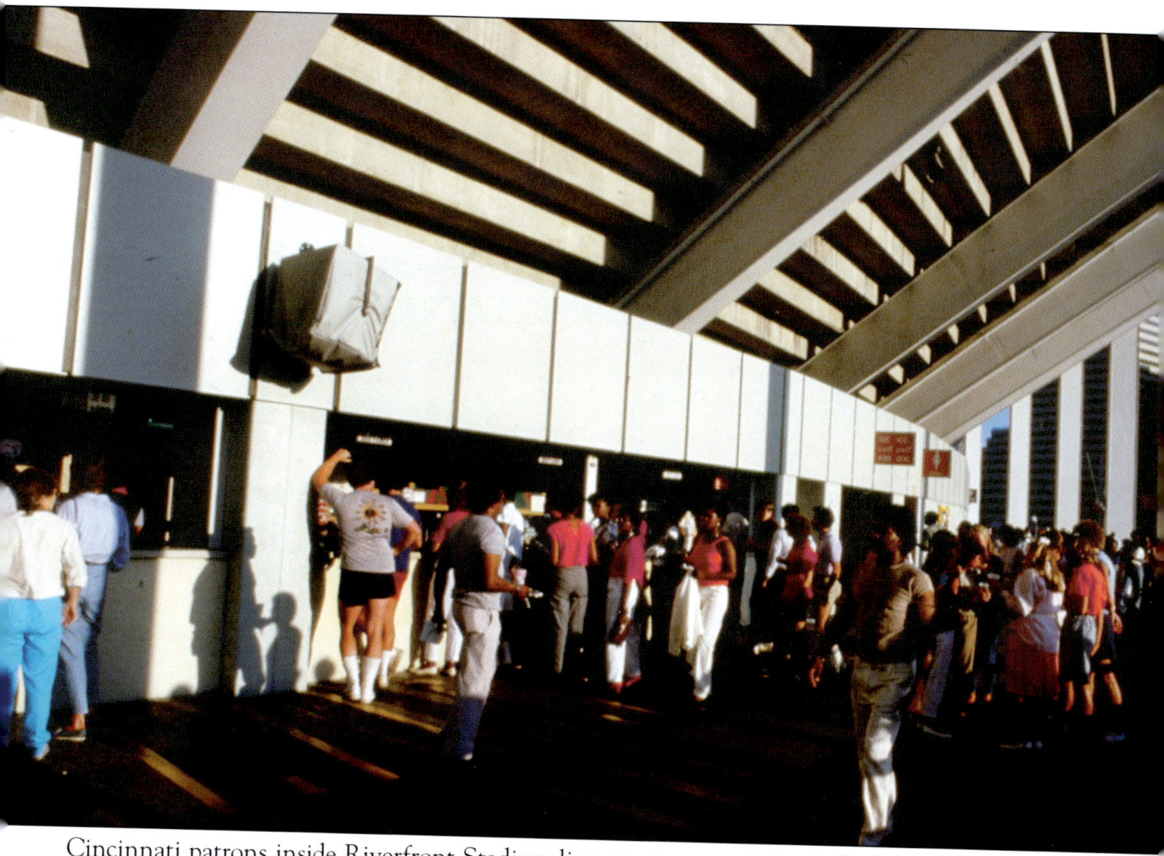

Cincinnati patrons inside Riverfront Stadium line up at concession stands designed primarily for sporting events. Large festival crowds attended performances that could begin as early as 7:30 p.m. and run as late as 1:00 a.m., and the stadium staff was well prepared to meet their needs from start to finish.

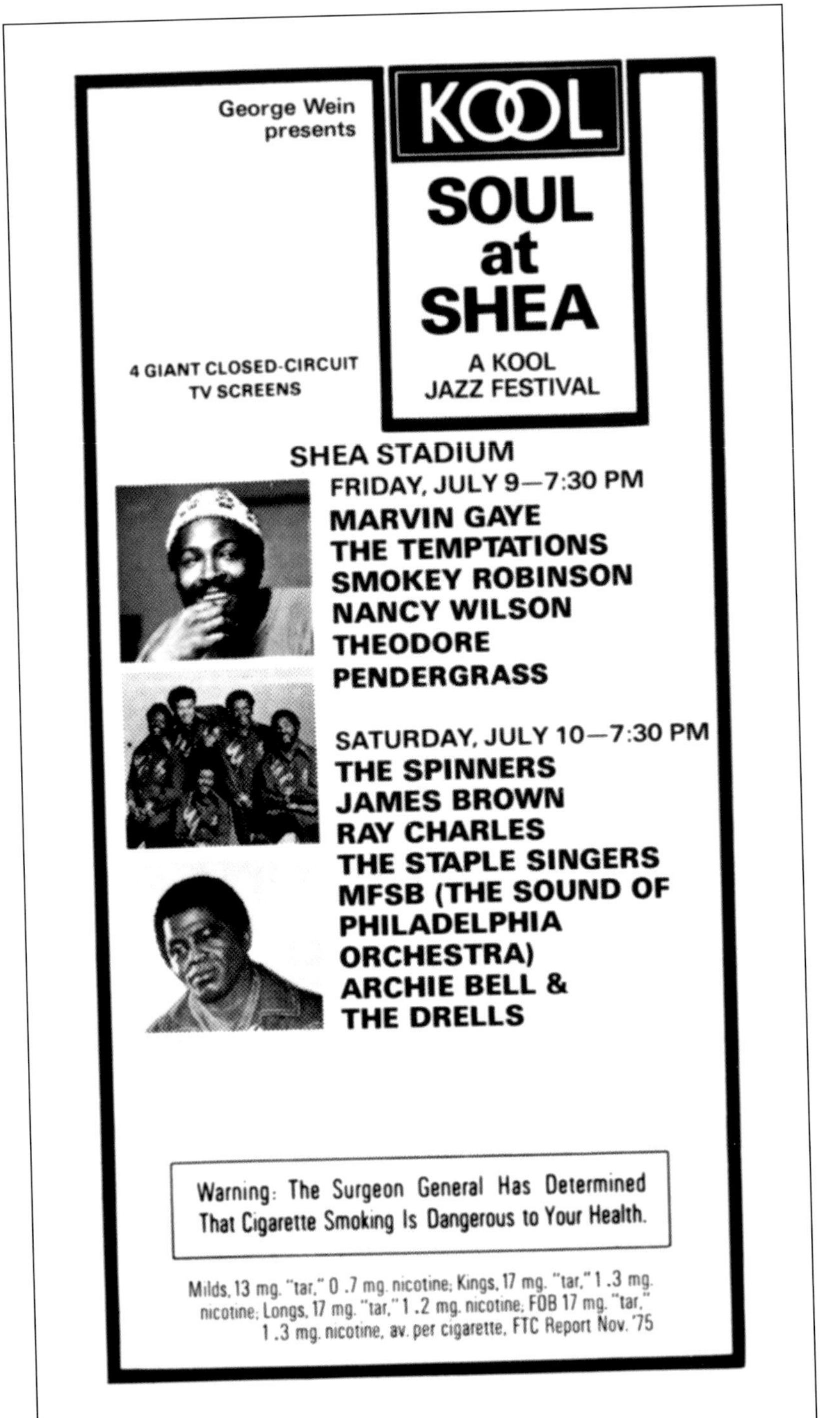

The festival would be presented under different banners in different cities. This advertising proof (or "slick") for the Kool Soul at Shea concert was used in advertisement placements promoting the event to be held at Shea Stadium (Flushing Meadows, Queens, New York). The incredible lineup is a snapshot of R&B music from that era.

The Surgeon General warnings on Kool Jazz Festival advertising, programs, and other media were a reminder of the inevitable fragility of cigarette sponsorships. While the necessary warnings were always present, the nature of the company's sponsorship permitted creative applications of the brand logo that arguably circumvented the regulations. In 1988, the tobacco industry, once considered the heavyweight champion of product liability lawsuits, negotiated the Tobacco Master Settlement Agreement in 46 states. The agreement specifically restricted advertising programs that targeted younger audiences, effectively ending cigarette company sponsorships of entertainment events.

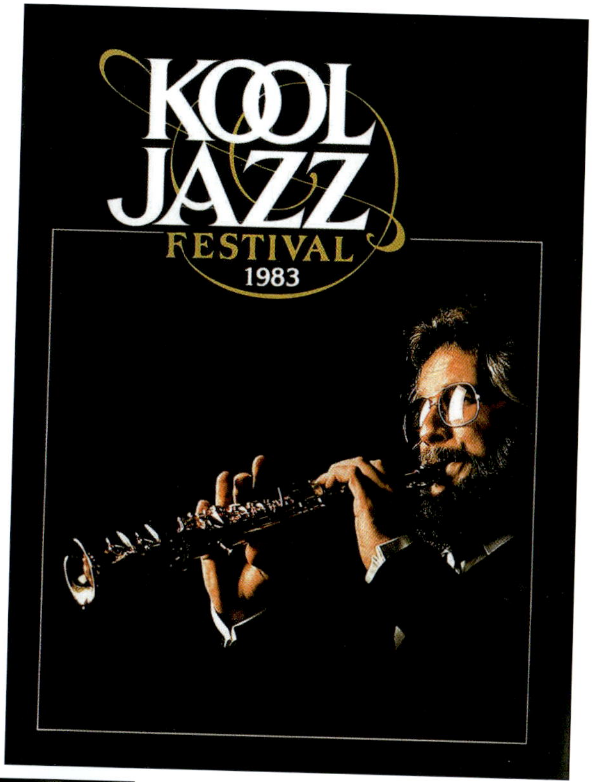

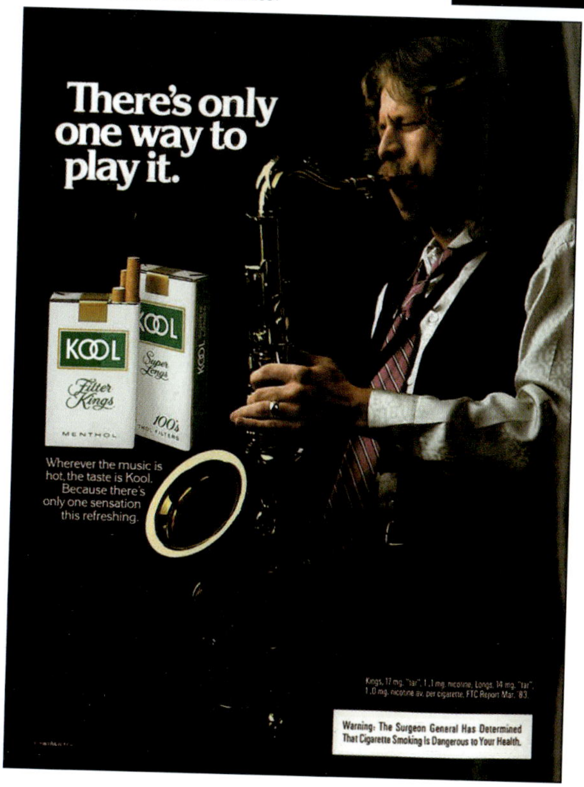

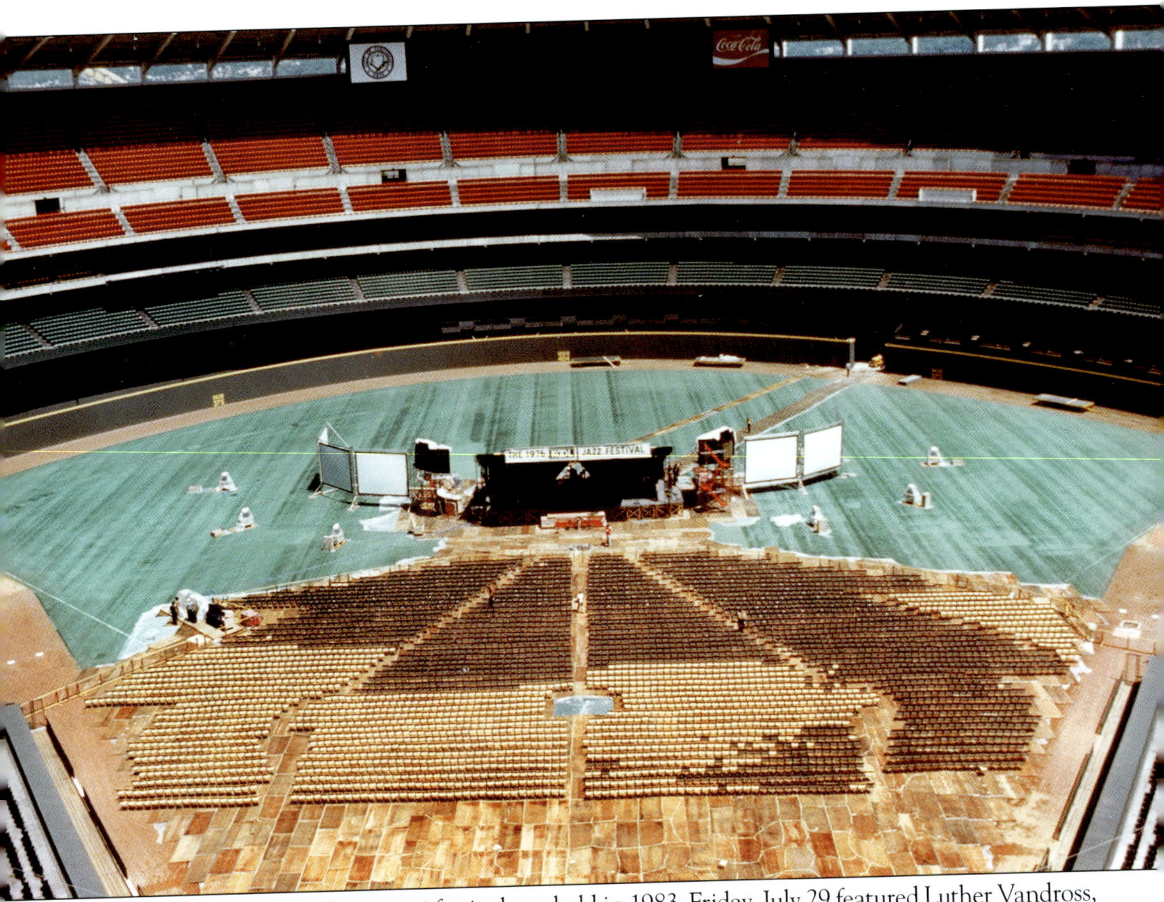

The 22nd year of the Cincinnati festival was held in 1983. Friday, July 29 featured Luther Vandross, the O'Jays, the Whispers, the Dazz Band, Cheryl Lynn, and the System. Saturday's show included Rick James, Lakeside, Cameo, Evelyn "Champagne" King, the Zapp Band, and Steve Arrington's Hall of Fame. This photograph shows the field setup nearly complete, with plywood protecting the valuable stadium turf and stage.

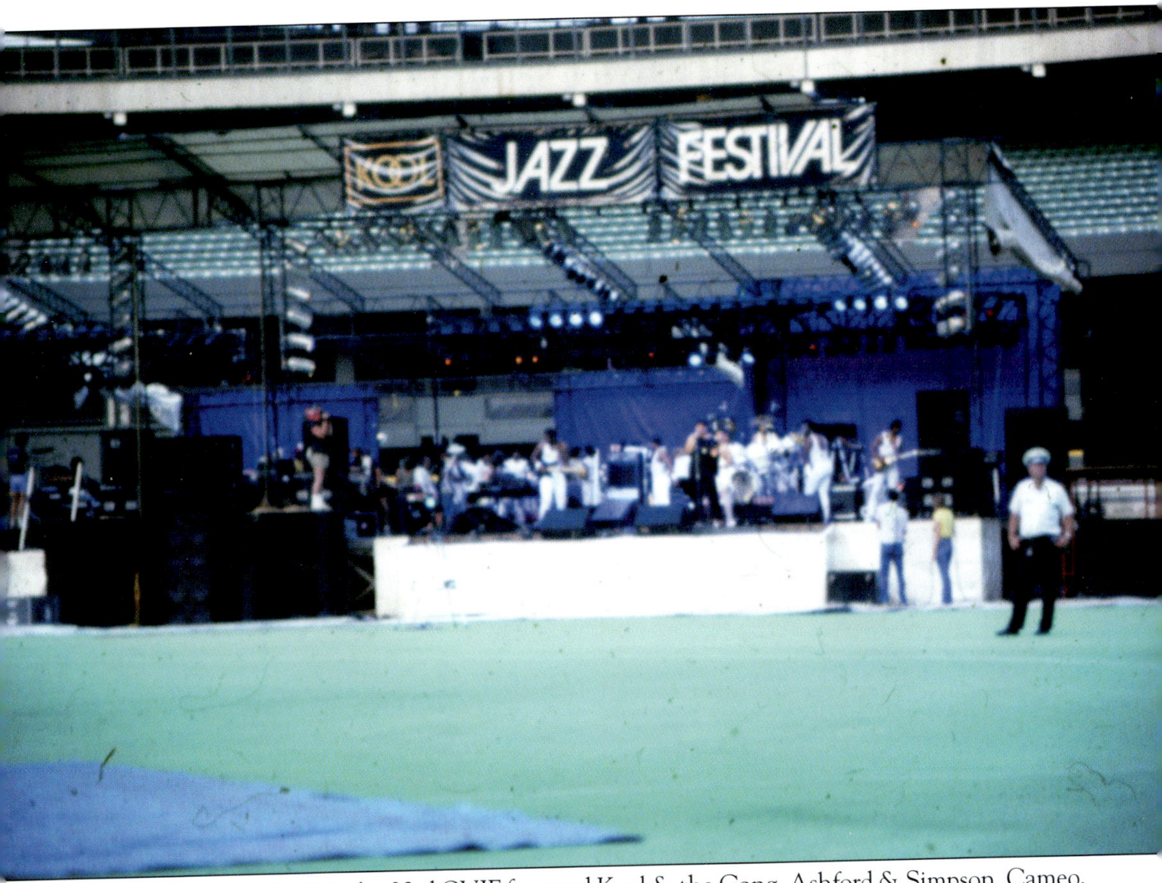

On Friday, July 27, 1984, the 23rd OVJF featured Kool & the Gang, Ashford & Simpson, Cameo, Midnight Star, and the Deele. Saturday's program starred Luther Vandross, Patti LaBelle, Maze featuring Frankie Beverly, Bobby Womack, and New Edition. Cincinnatians Antonio "LA" Reid and the Deele were honored to be included. Reid said, "We're all pretty excited about it. For us, this is the show of all shows . . . I never thought I'd be sharing the stage with Kool & the Gang." His excitement was shared by an estimated 500 friends and family who came to see them play.

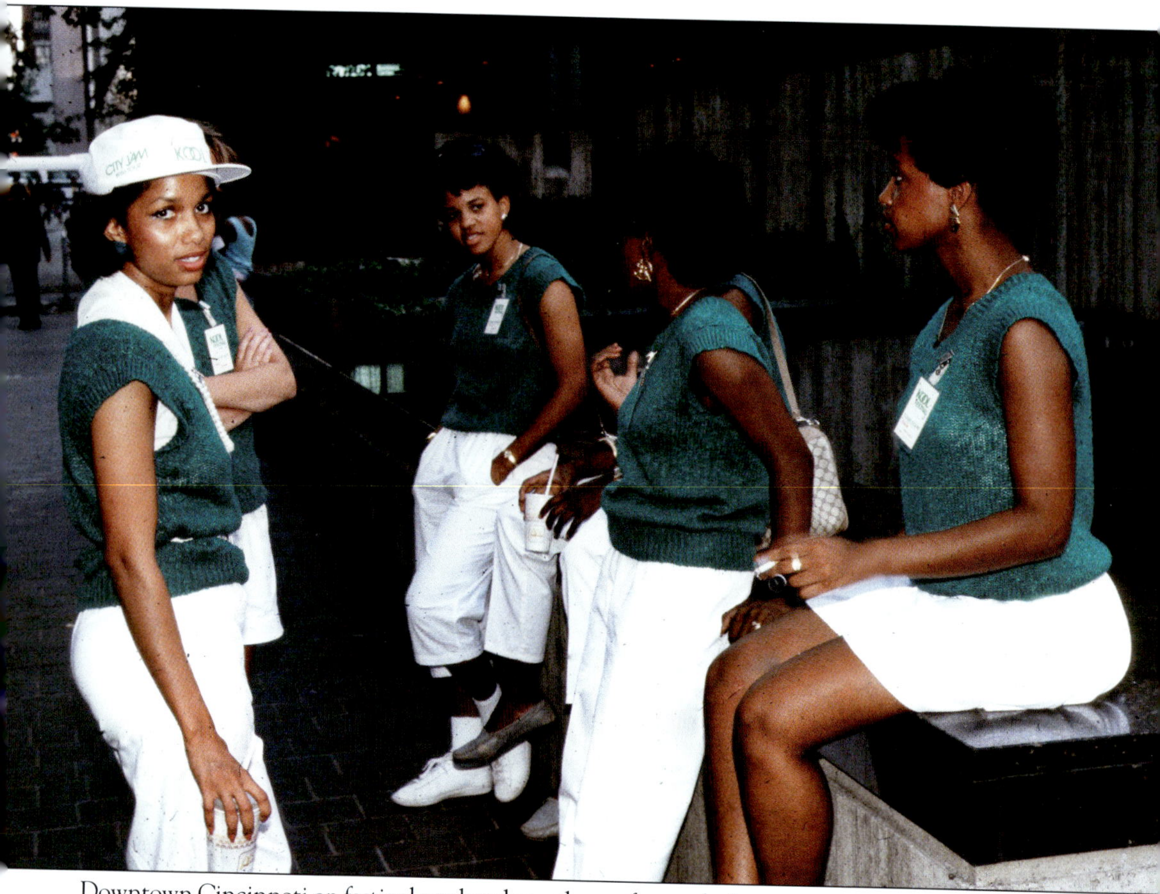

Downtown Cincinnati on festival weekend was the perfect end-of-summer getaway for visitors from out of town. As the national program began to contract, Cincinnati maintained its popularity as a destination. The photograph shows festival event promotions staff taking a break from the nearby free concert being held at Cincinnati's Fountain Square.

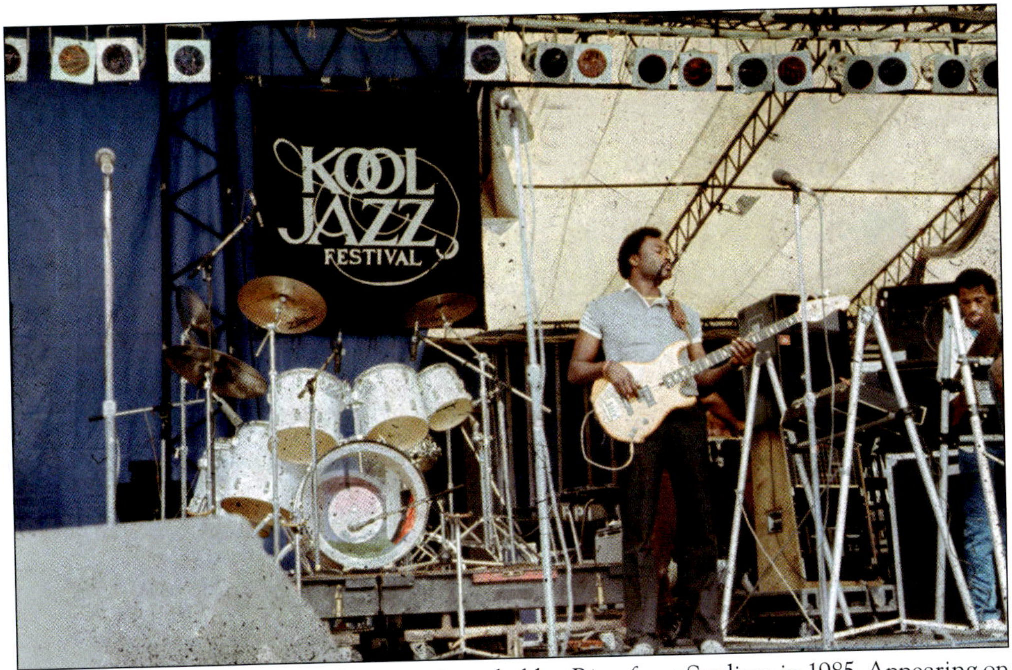

The 24th Kool Jazz Festival in Cincinnati was held at Riverfront Stadium in 1985. Appearing on Friday, July 27 were Luther Vandross, the Commodores, Teena Marie, Shalamar, and the Dazz Band. Saturday's concert featured the Gap Band, Jeffrey Osborne, Patti LaBelle, Midnight Star, and Evelyn "Champagne" King.

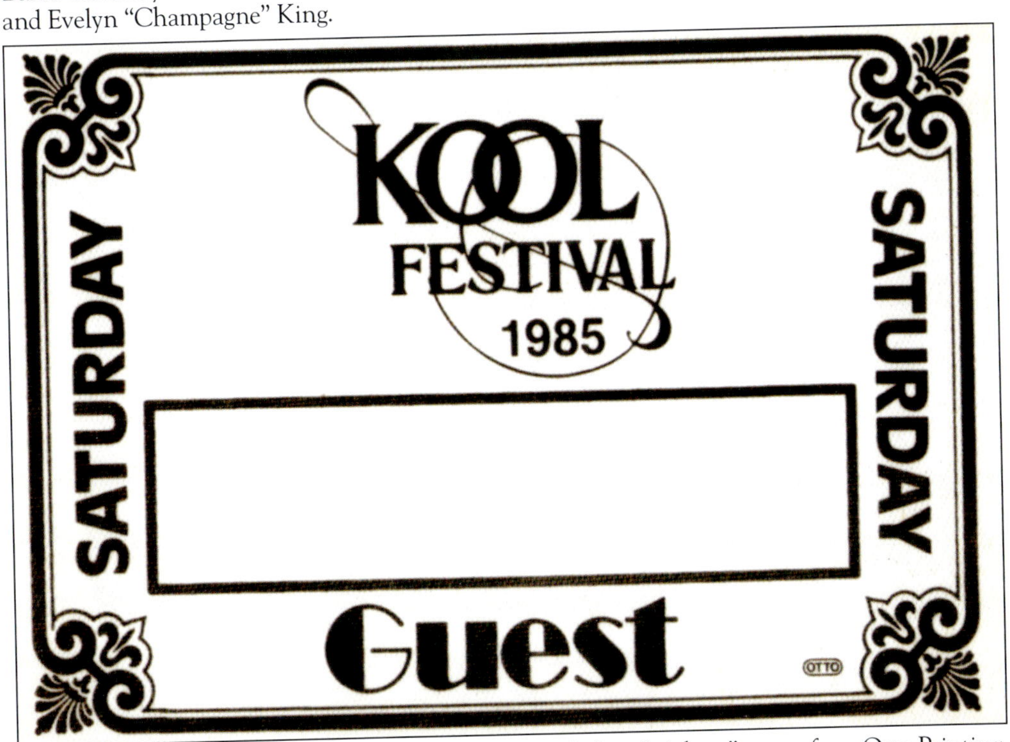

Backstage identification now came in many forms, including "stick on" passes from Otto Printing, state of the art at the time.

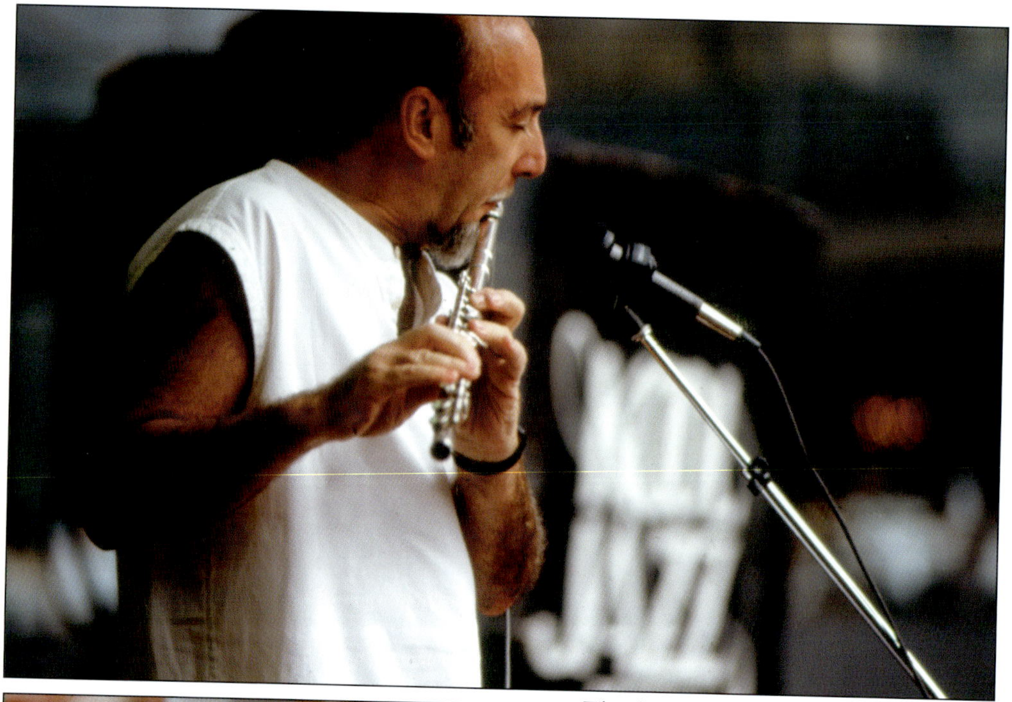

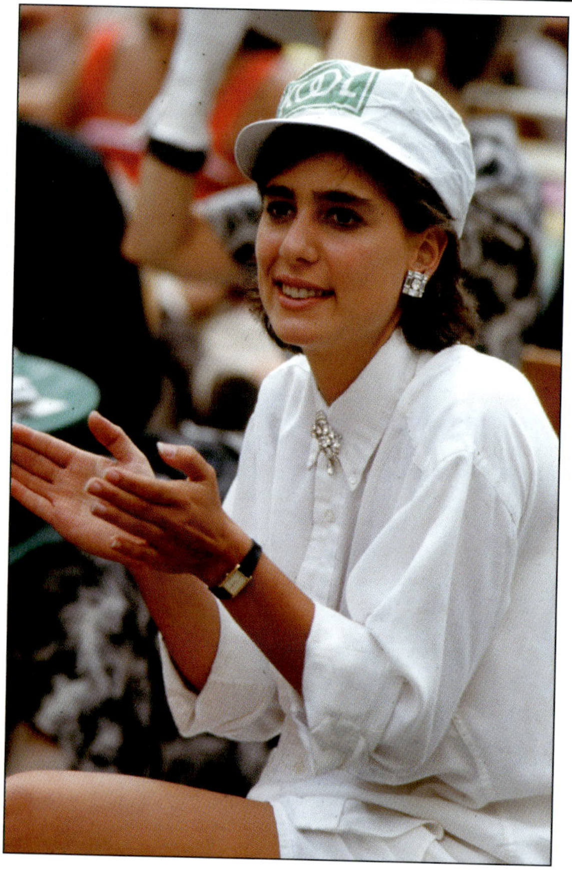

The festival had moved away from its jazz roots in response to the trends in popular music, but jazz artists continued to be featured in festival lineups, at promotional and community events, and through special tours. Herbie Mann, shown above in 1985, performs at one of the Cincinnati free concerts held at Fountain Square. Dino Santangelo's daughter Nancy (left) coordinated public relations and marketing and is shown in the audience, taking a break to enjoy the show.

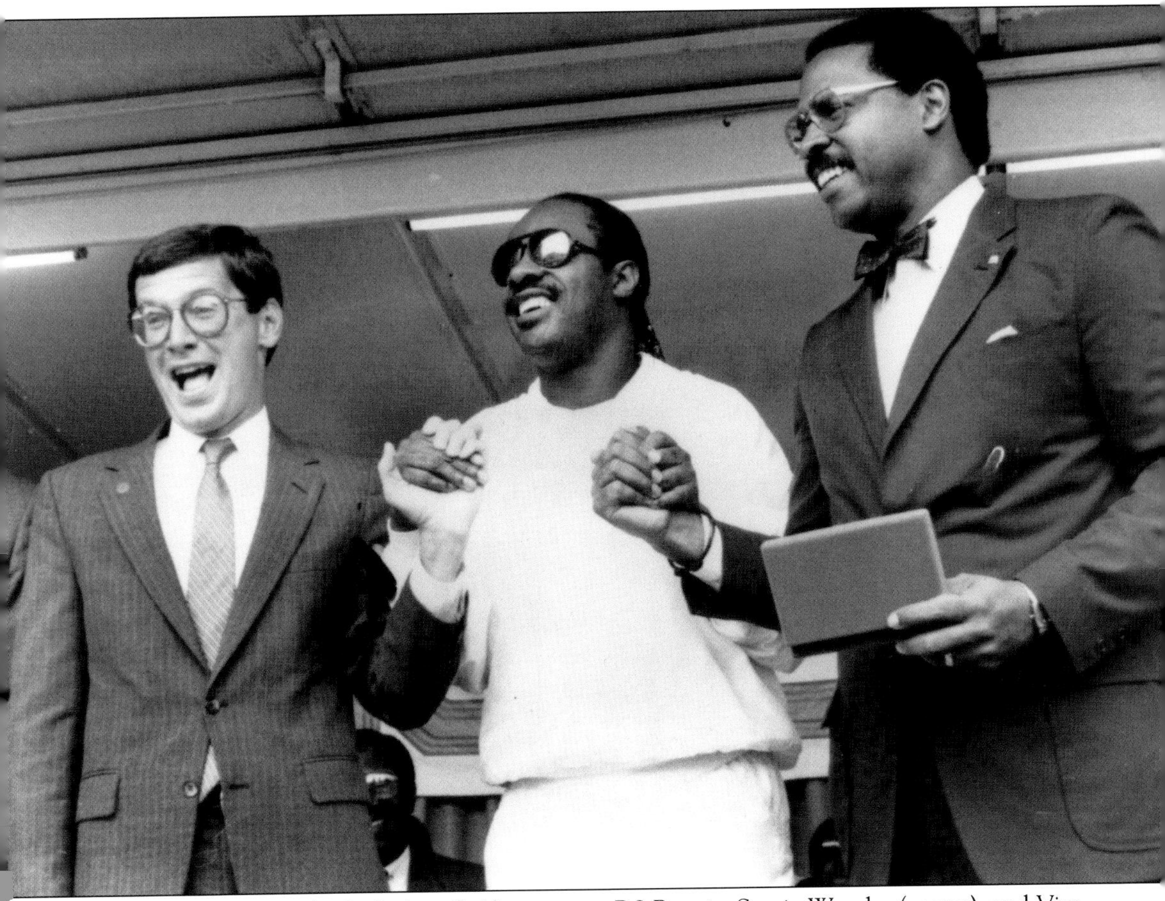

Cincinnati mayor Charlie Luken (left), superstar R&B artist Stevie Wonder (center), and Vice-Mayor Ken Blackwell (right) link hands in bipartisan solidarity as Wonder is presented with a key to the City of Cincinnati. The Cincinnati festival became an annual opportunity for politicians to celebrate the universal appeal of music and the positive economic impacts for their community.

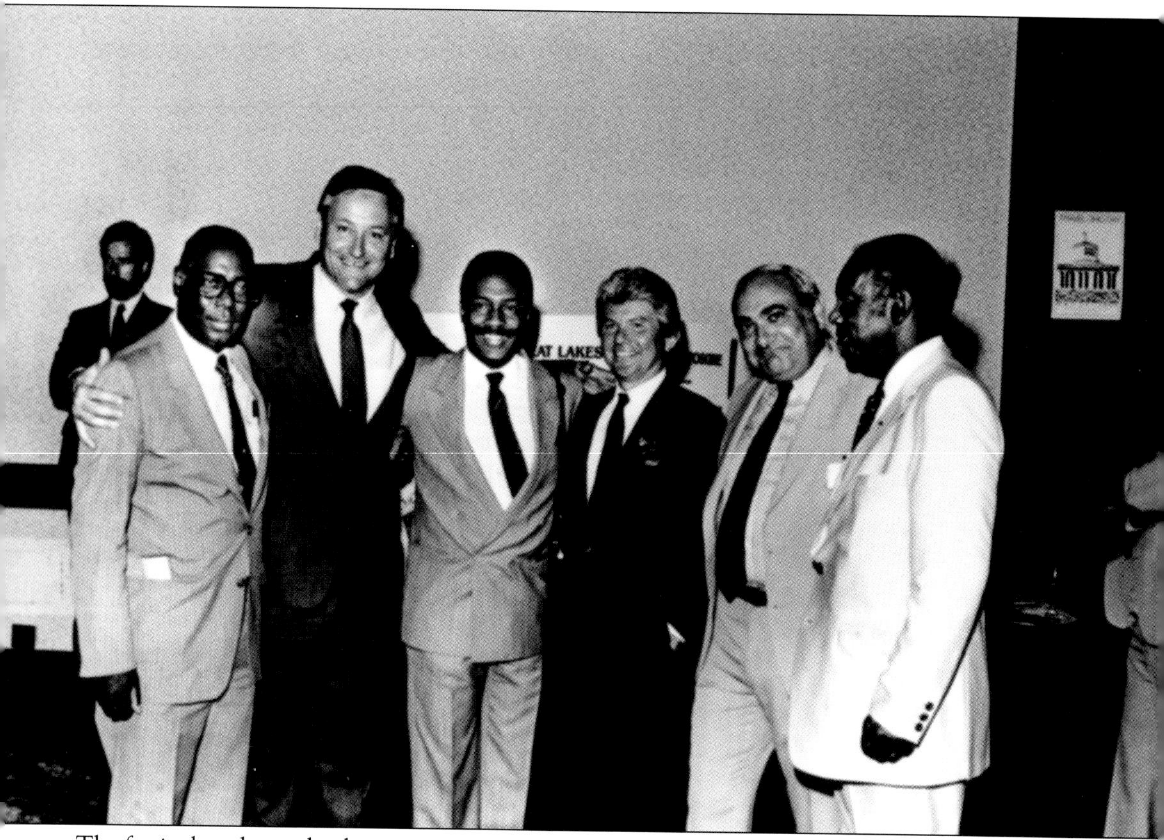

The festival made good politics, crossing aisles and racial lines. Dick Celeste, Ohio's governor the year the Cincinnati festival turned 25, noted that "the association between the Kool Festival and the 'Ohio The Heart Of It All' campaign is one that is welcomed." Shown in the photograph are, from left to right (omitting the governor's aide in the left background), Sen. William Mallory, Governor Celeste, Cincinnati businessman Steve Reece, state senator Stanley Aronoff, Dino Santangelo, and state representative C.J. McLin.

Seven

1986

The Festival Lives On

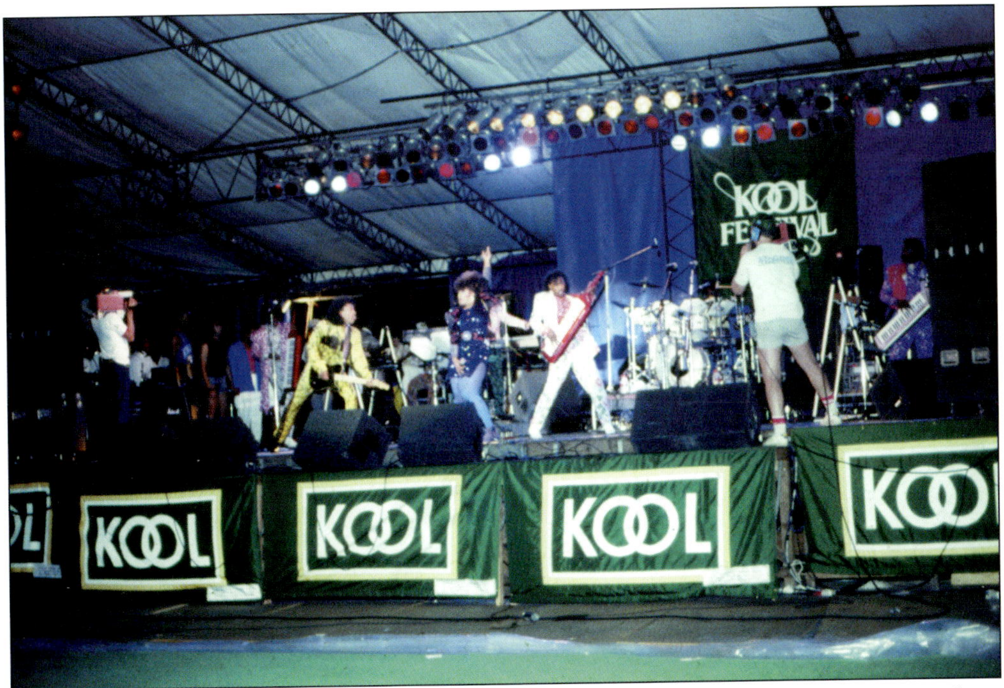

The year 1986 marked the festival's silver anniversary, and the lineup for the event at Riverfront Stadium reflected the occasion. Appearing on Friday, August 1 were New Edition, Jennifer Holliday, Cherrelle, Rene and Angela, Zapp, Starpoint, and Sly Fox. Saturday's performers included Luther Vandross, Natalie Cole, Maze featuring Frankie Beverly, Midnight Star, Klymaxx, the S.O.S. Band, and Cash Flow. Tickets cost $18.50, $15.50, and $12. Response from fans to the announcement of the lineup was said to be "overwhelming," according to festival officials.

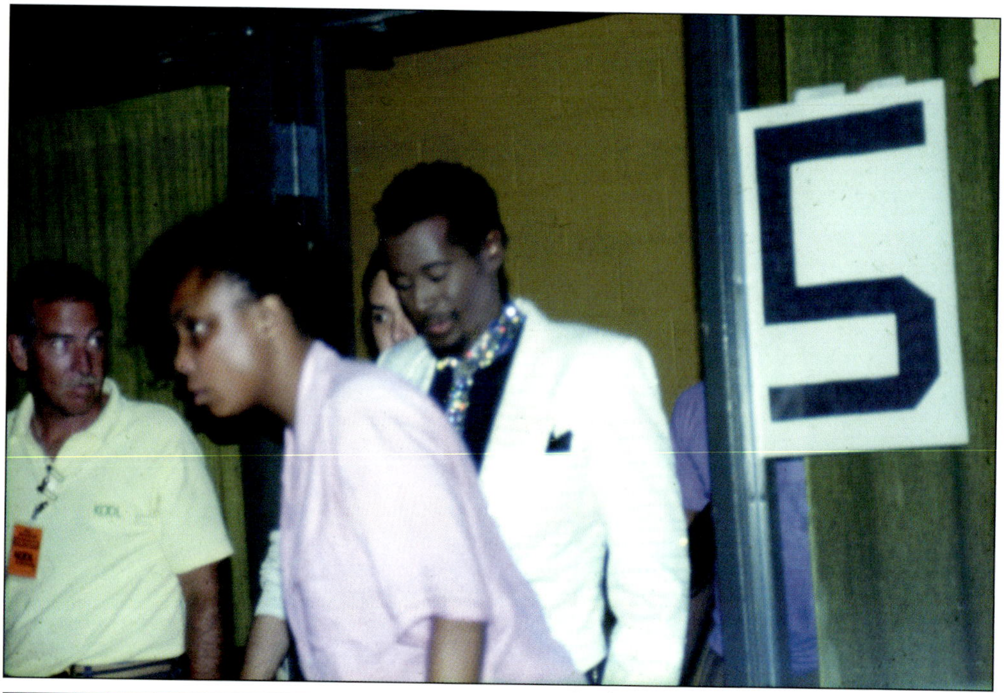

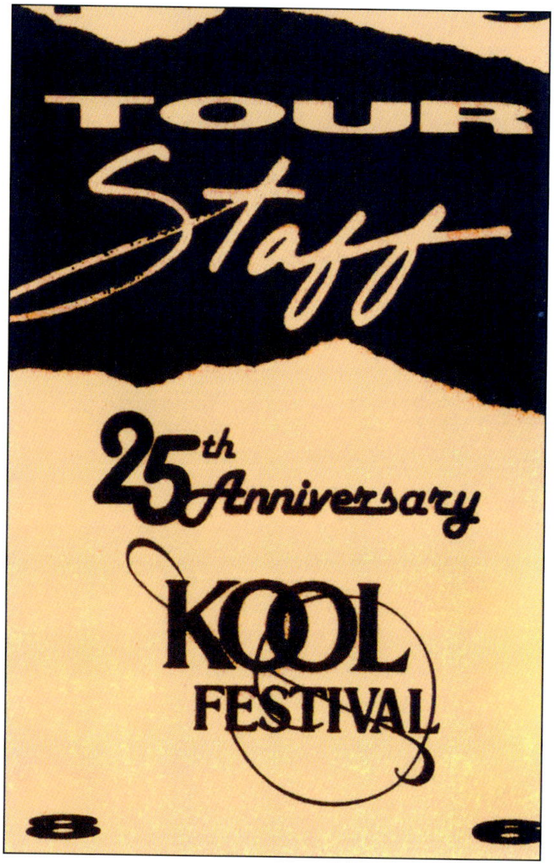

Luther Vandross (above, white jacket) commanded the highest fee of any artist at the 1985 festival, earning $100,000 out of a total entertainment budget of $350,000. What most people did not realize was that Vandross had actually been unavailable, having recently concluded his own tour. But upon hearing it was the Cincinnati festival's 25th anniversary, he wired Dino Santangelo to confirm his appearance. Steve Schildmeyer (above, left) was one of the festival's most experienced line producers. At left is that year's tour identification laminate worn by staff during the festival's 25th anniversary.

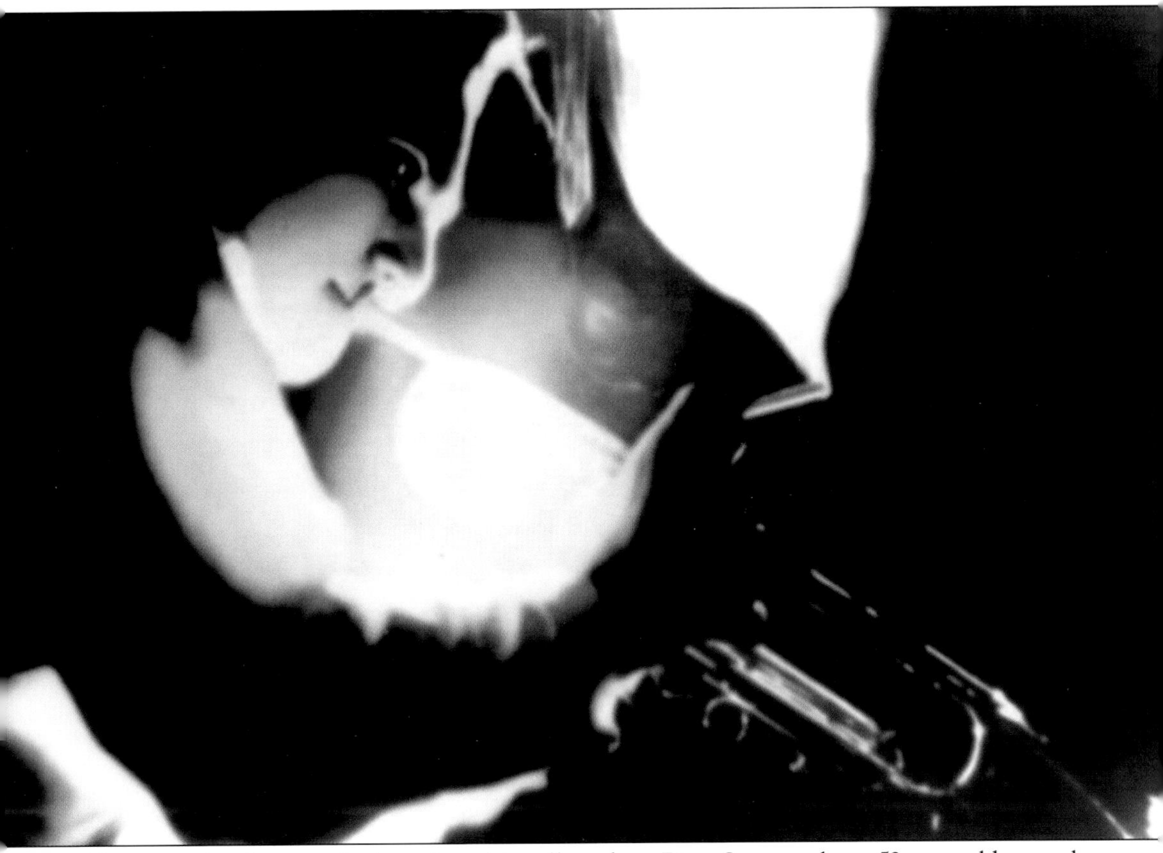

Shown in the photograph above from his college days, Dino Santangelo, at 52 years old, passed away in his sleep just weeks before the silver anniversary of the festival he had created. Jerry Springer, then anchor for News 5, memorialized Santangelo on his program: "What was not said, but easily observed, was that the Kool Festival, in terms of audience, was a black festival. In conservative Cincinnati, a number of institutions seemed to have had trouble with that. . . . There would be hotel memos saying, 'Don't put out the good towels, watch the silverware' . . . and a host of other racist reactions to this largely black event, the sum of which seemed to indicate more of a community resistance to the affair than an open-arm welcome. But Santangelo stuck with it and the city learned to accept it and then like it and finally promote it. . . . On this 25th anniversary of a wonderful success story, we know something not only about the festival but about the man who created it . . . that his best music was neither jazz nor rhythm and blues, but rather harmony . . . racial harmony."

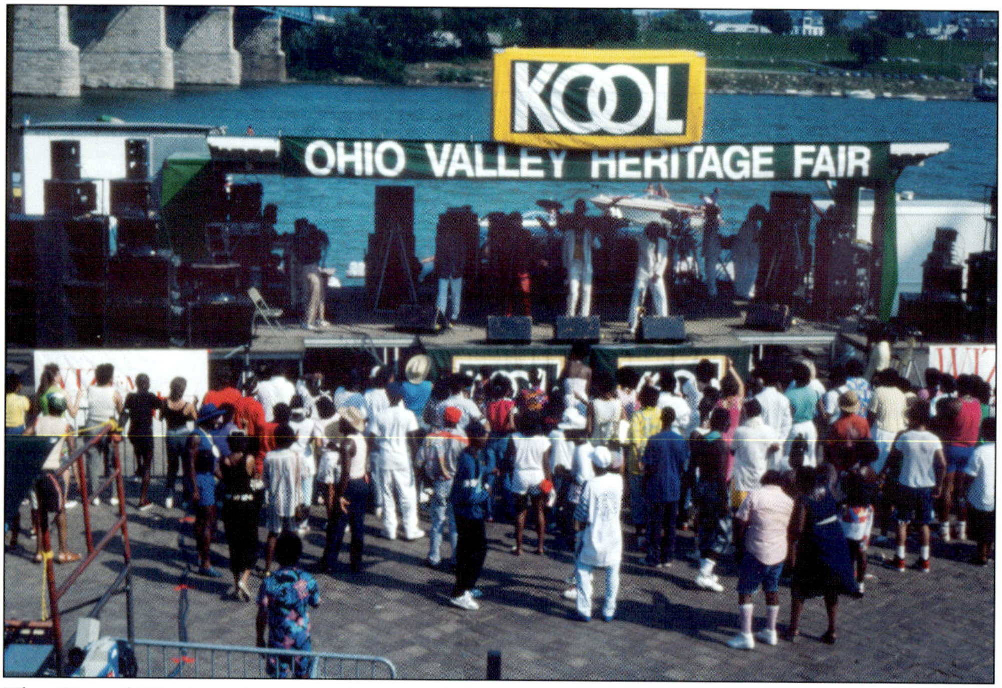

The City of Cincinnati managed many of the venues that hosted festival community events. The Serpentine Wall along the Ohio River was near Riverfront Stadium and a perfect setting for the Ohio Valley Heritage Fair in 1987. Inaugurated as a community celebration of past, present, and future, the fair combined music with food, art, and families, showcasing the city to thousands of visitors. The photograph below shows Cincinnati Recreation Commission director Tony Proccacino.

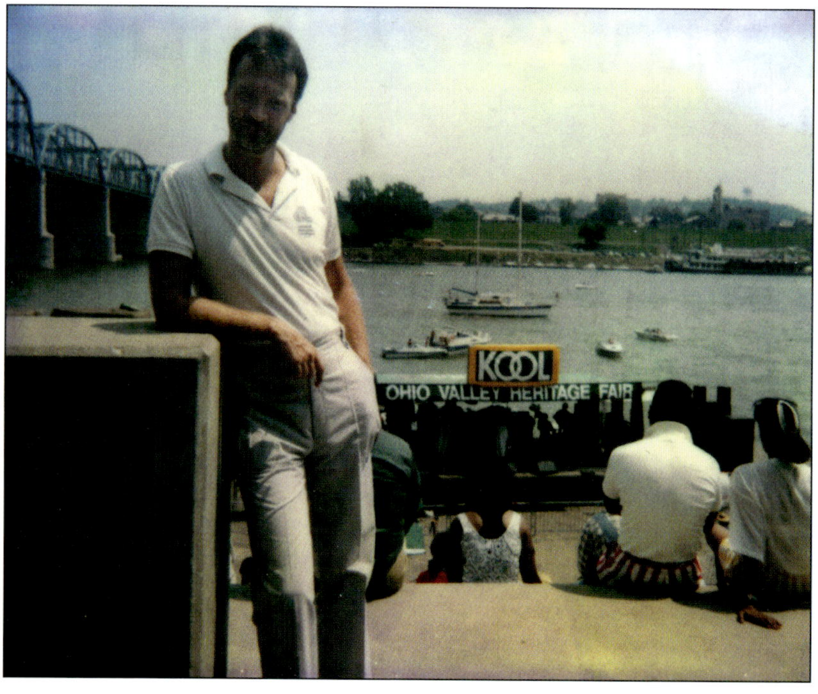

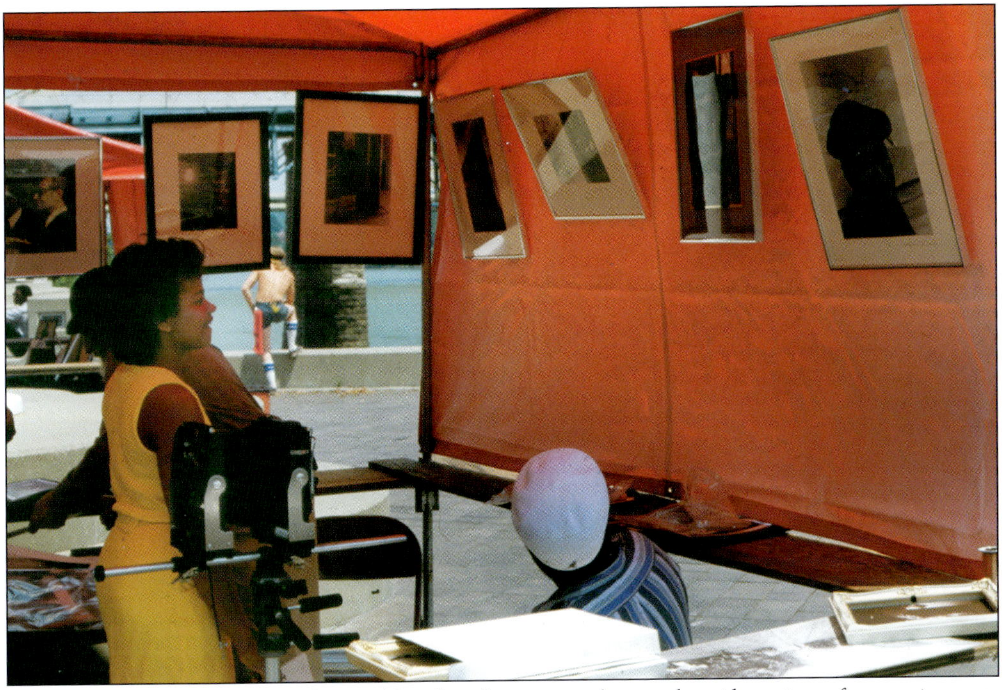

The Ohio Valley Heritage Fair featured local craftsmen, vendors, and a wide variety of entertainments for festival visitors and locals alike. The photograph below shows one of the event participants, "Percy," for whom every button, pin, and item on his clothing represented a story he knew or an experience he would share. Children were his best customers, and young people gathered to hear his storytelling.

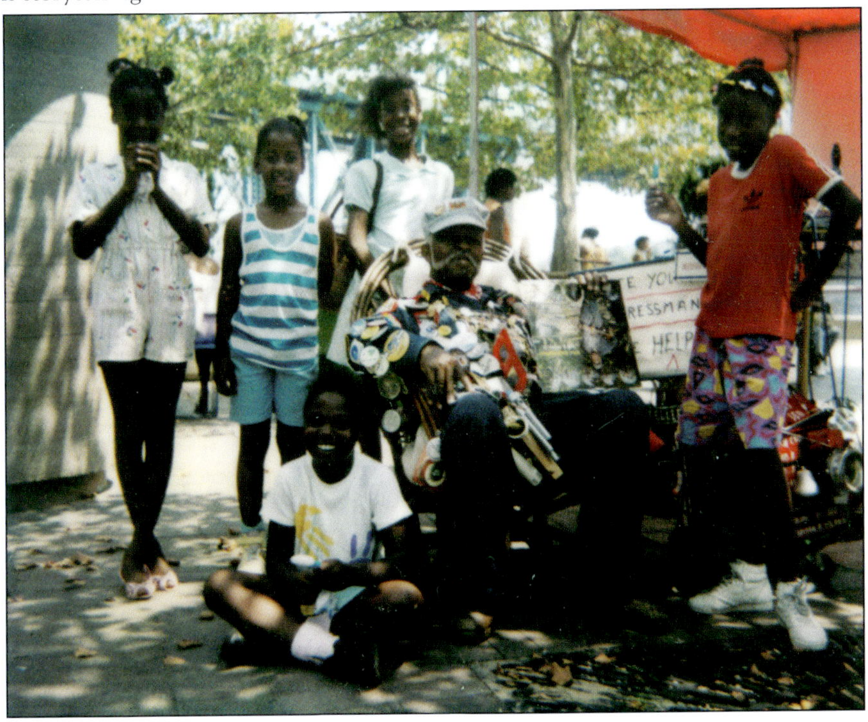

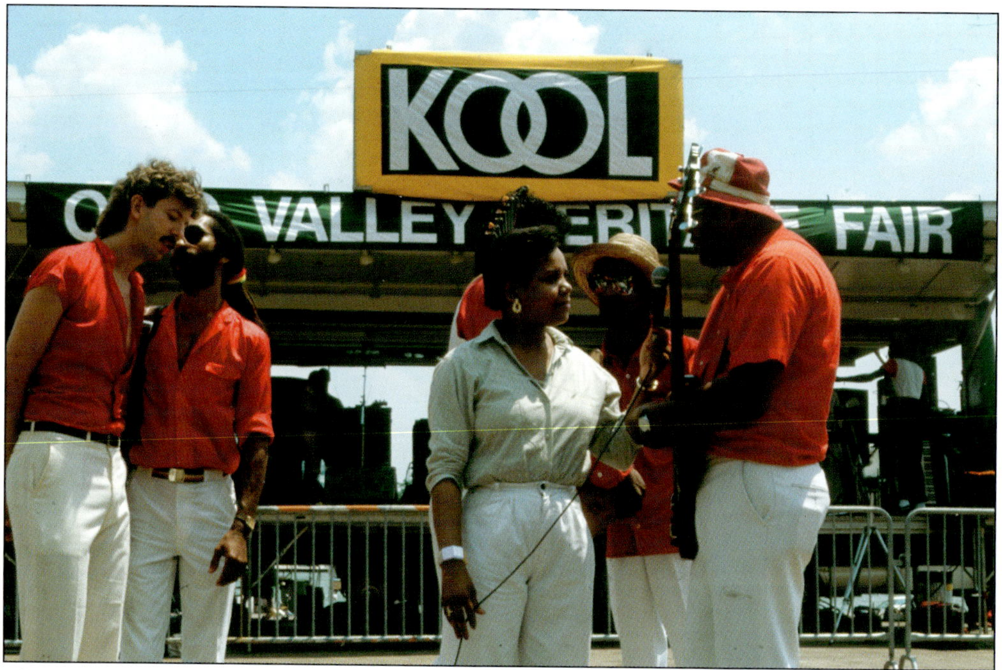

The city's support for the festival in Cincinnati had come full circle, and the event was embraced as an end-of-summer tradition. In the photograph above, performers thank a representative of the Cincinnati Recreation Commission. In the photograph below, Tabatha Anderson (center) was that year's winner of the Miss Black Cincinnati Pageant and is shown accompanied by the founder of the pageant, Robert Humphries (left), and an unidentified man (right).

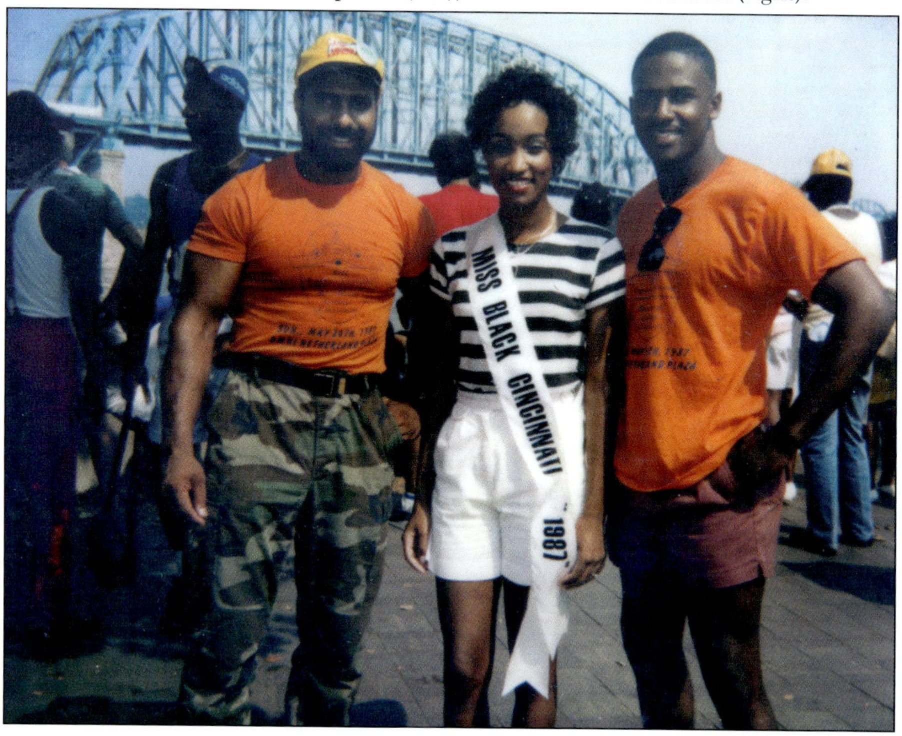

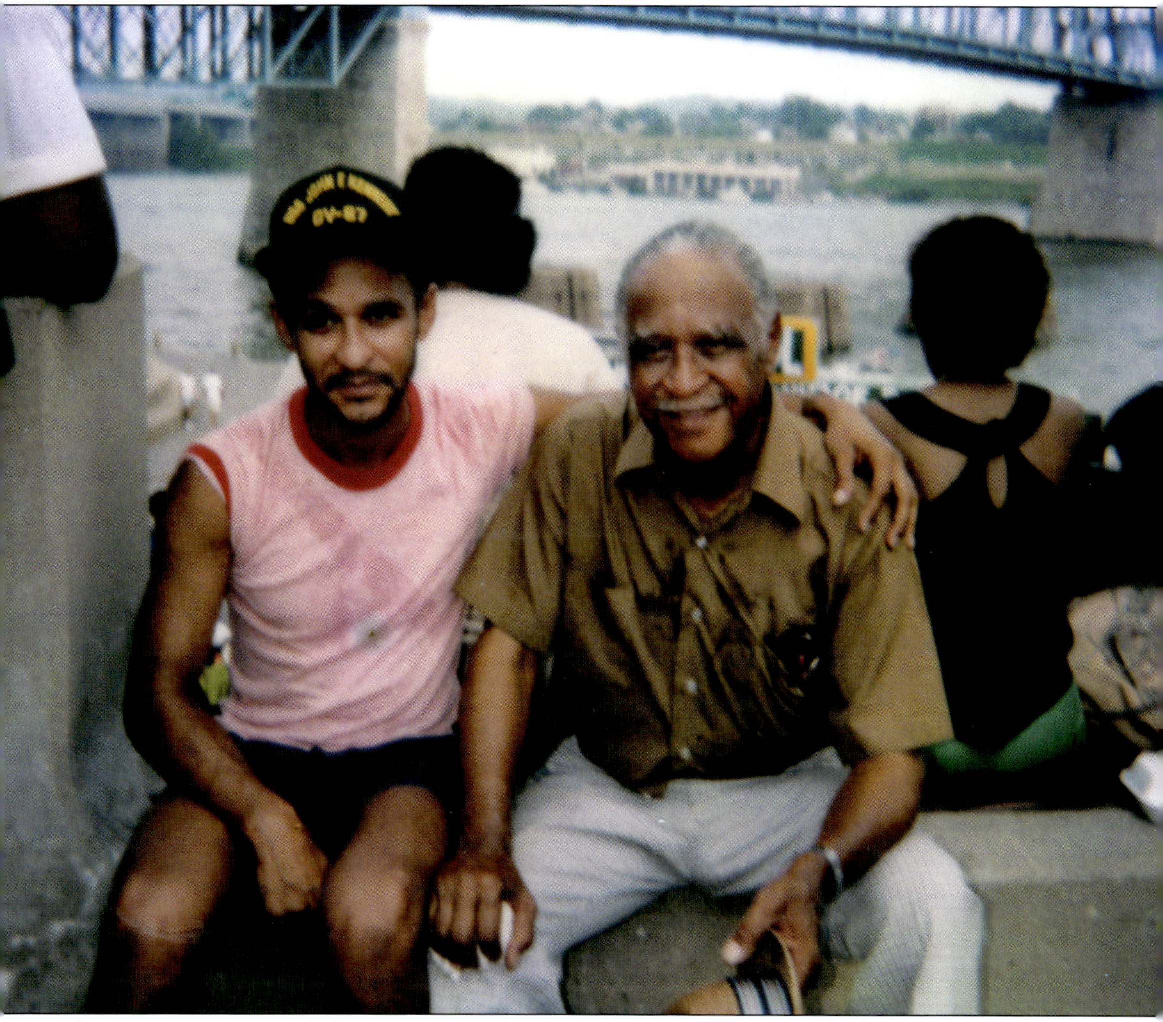

The Heritage Fair provided an opportunity for different generations to come together outside of the stadium concerts and celebrate their achievements as a community (an anonymous father and son are shown here at the Serpentine Wall). It was a fitting tribute to Dino Santangelo, whose career exemplified working collaboratively and who "fostered a spirit of cooperation that was a major factor in the success of his numerous projects," according to a resolution of the Ohio Senate. Santangelo was also a posthumous recipient of the NAACP Brotherhood Award "in recognition of his generous support and for his longstanding commitment to the high ideals of brotherhood in the Cincinnati community and in the nation." A memorial fund with the University of Cincinnati's College-Conservatory of Music was founded in Santangelo's memory to recognize and support outstanding jazz studies majors.

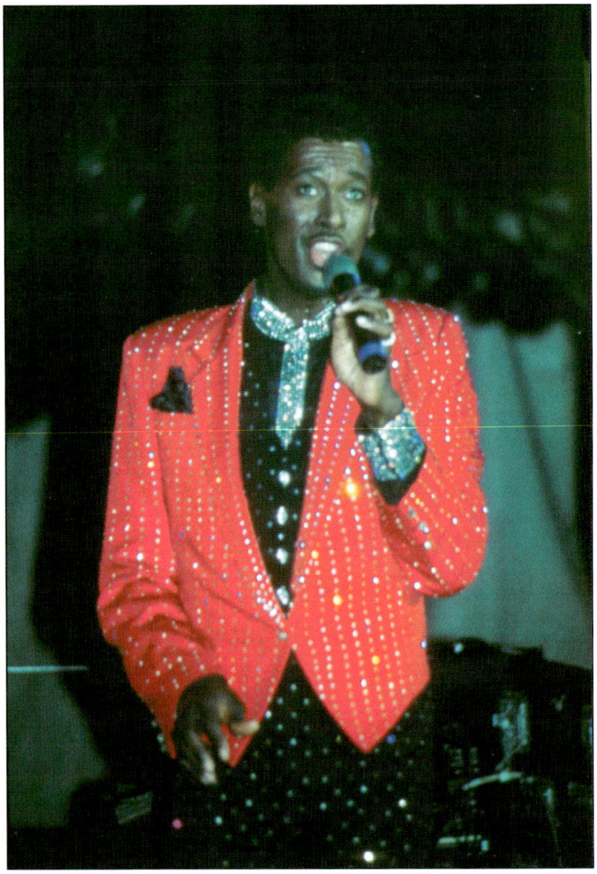

The 1987 festival tour would be the last to be sponsored by Kool—the end of an era in the entertainment industry. But the show would go on, and the depth of support for the Cincinnati event was an affirmation of the deep and lasting connections forged by its late founder and a community of dedicated fans throughout the region. Superstars Luther Vandross (left) and Patti LaBelle (below, left) would headline the lineups that year.

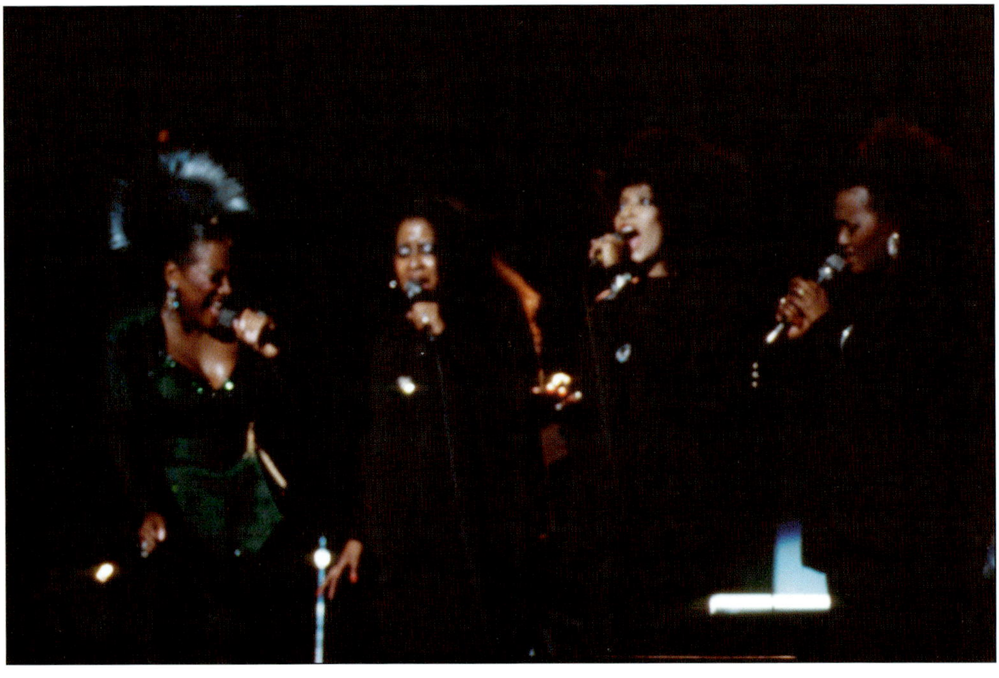

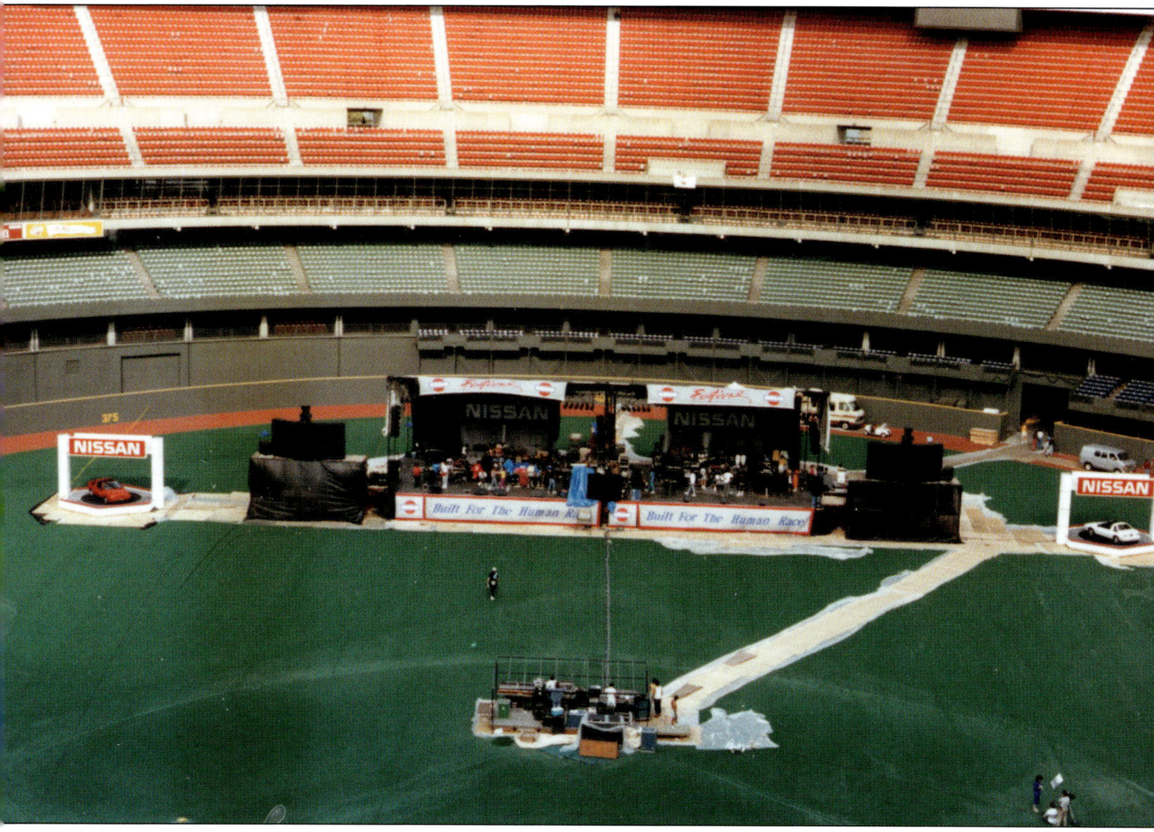

While sponsors would continue to change over the ensuing years, the festival remains an established tradition that to this day marks the end of summer in Cincinnati. From its Newport Jazz Festival roots, the Cincinnati festival grew to become its own unique event, delighting diverse audiences and providing the community an annual opportunity to welcome tens of thousands of visitors.